Yingele Nit Vein

"Boy, Don't Cry"

Memories of a Jewish child, 1939-1945

Lodz Ghetto
Auschwitz / Birkenau
Dachau
Kaufering
Landsberg

Bernard Marks

Marks, Bernard
    Yiingele Nit Vein; "Boy, Don't Cry" : Memories of a Jewish Child, 1939-1945.

Photographs courtesy of Bernard Marks;
    U.S. Army Archives
    United States Holocaust Memorial Museum
    Berlin Archives
    Jewish Museum, Frankfurt, Yad Vashem Photo Archive,
Photographer: Walter Genewein (SS Officer)

ISBN: 978-1-941125-00-7

Library of Congress Control Number: 2013918831

Printed in the United States by

I Street Press
Sacramento Public Library
828 I Street
Sacramento, CA 95814

Cover Design by Gerald F. Ward

6 7 8 9

Dedication

This book is dedicated to my dear father Josef, my "angel", who managed for five-and-a-half years during the Holocaust to outwit the Nazis in order to save my life, and to my dear wife Eleanor (Ellie) Cohen Marks, who shared most of her life with me and with whom I was very happily married for fifty-six years.

Bernard Marks

Introduction

The Voice of A Survivor

In his book, "Yingele Nit Vein (Boy Don't Cry): Memories of a Jewish Child from 1939 to 1945," Bernard Marks recounts a childhood spent in the Lodz Ghetto, in the notorious extermination camp of Auschwitz-Birkenau and in the satellite concentration camps of Dachau near Landsberg am Lech, Bavaria. Bernard Marks was born as Ber Makowski in the Polish city of Lodz. It was here where he spent his early years, loved and cared for in a large Jewish family. The Makowskis were part of the approximately 233,000 Jews who lived in Lodz in 1939. With its burgeoning textile industry as well as a rich tradition of Jewish life and culture, Lodz was a modern city ranked second in size only to Warsaw, Poland.

As described by Israel Joshua Singer in his 1937 novel, "The Brothers Ashkenazi" "Lodz seethed in ferment as the city grew day by day, hour by hour. Strangers converged from all over: German engineers and master weavers; English chemists, designers and patternmakers; Russian merchant princes in blue coats and wide trousers over short patent-leather boots; Jewish traveling salesmen and commission agents –

gay, lusty young men who descended upon Lodz to make money and have fun."

Since the earliest times, Lodz has played a central part in Poland's history. The city is located on the edge of the Lodz Highlands, at the watershed of the Vistula and Oder rivers, about eighty miles southwest of the capital city of Warsaw. One of the visual elements incorporated into Lodz's coat-of-arms is a boat, which is the meaning of the name in the Polish language, hinting that the town would one day become a major center for commerce.

The first written mention of the village of Lodzia appears in an ecclesiastical document dated 1332. By the sixteenth century, most of the town's 800 inhabitants were employed in agricultural pursuits, raising grain on surrounding farms. Until the 1700s, the town was a stopping point on the trade route between the regions of Masovia to the east on the border with Russia, and Silesia, with its wealth of mineral resources, located to the southwest along the Oder River.

Because of it geographic location, diverse mix of cultures, lack of a centralized government and outside political influences, control of the town remained fluid for the following several centuries, from a Prussian dependency in 1793 to the Duchy of Warsaw in 1806, to Russian control by 1815. Mirroring the great Industrial Revolution that was taking place across Western Europe at the time, in 1820 a movement was afoot to turn the small town into a hub of industry. By the 1830s, the steady influx of artisans and traders and the town's skilled labor pool had transformed Lodz into the premier textile producer of the entire Russian empire. That, in turn, drew more immigrants to Lodz from all across Europe, logically from southern Germany and Bohemia, but also from Ireland, England, France and Portugal. Three ethnic groups comprised the bulk of the city's residents: the indigenous Poles, Germans and Jews. These dominant populations also contributed heavily to Lodz's development, both business-wise and culturally.

The 19th century saw the city's population virtually explodes, doubling every decade between 1823 and 1870. In 1850, the burgeoning Russian market was opened up to Lodz when that country abolished trade restrictions and, in 1865, the first rail line was opened, linking Lodz with Warsaw and other large markets. Before long, Lodz had grown to become the second largest city in Poland. By the last decade of the century, it also was the scene of a growing cultural community of writers, poets, artists and musicians, home to such future luminaries as pianist Arthur Rubenstein and others.

As the factories continued their industrialization, labor leaders saw the need for organization and in 1892, a massive strike shut down most of the plants, paralyzing much of the output of goods. Thirteen years later, during the Lodz Insurrection or "June Days" of 1905, more than 300 workers were killed when czarist police moved in to put down the revolution. However, despite such civil unrest and the threat of war clouds gathering on the horizon, by the outbreak of World

War One in 1914, Lodz was one of the most densely populated industrial cities in the world with a population of well over 200,000. About one in three residents was Jewish.

Lodz had become widely renowned as the "Manchester of Poland" for its many textile mills, 175 of which were owned by Jews. Since the mid-19th century, Lodz's Jewish residents had been free to live anywhere in the city they wished but many chose to remain in the traditional Jewish quarter known as the "Old City."

During the Great War, Lodz came under German occupation. Much of the city, including many factories, were destroyed in the fighting. With the end of that conflict, it was returned to Poland yet one didn't have to look far to see that times were changing. The Bolshevik Revolution of 1917 and subsequent civil war in Russia ended Lodz's profitable trade with the East. They were followed by a war with Germany that effectively closed off Western markets to Polish-made textiles. Then came more workers' protests and even riots. The worldwide Great Depression further exacerbated the already volatile situation during the 1930s.

The city's formerly peaceful way of life was not destined to last.

During the period between the first and second World Wars, anti-Jewish sentiment, as well as repressive policies instituted by German political agitators, began surfacing. Into this maelstrom of unrest was born a boy named Ber Makowski on September 17th, 1932. It was a joyous day for his family.

But the uncertainty that accompanied Adolph Hitler's rise to power as Chancellor of Germany in March of 1933 culminated in vicious anti-Semitic pogroms in that country during 1933, 1934 and 1935, in which many Jews were killed. By 1938, Heinrich Himmler's SS storm troopers were arresting wealthy German Jews, and Nazi military guards were placed outside Jewish-owned businesses to prevent non-Jews from patronizing them.

Then, on the night of September 9, 1938, every Jews' worst nightmare came true. Whipped to a frenzy by lies and propaganda from Josef Goebbels, Hitler's Minister of Public Enlightenment, gangs of Nazi followers ran rampant, roaming the streets of German cities and towns; smashing and vandalizing synagogues, homes and Jewish-owned shops; raping, beating and torturing their victims. Twenty thousand men were shipped off to torture and likely death in concentration camps. The following morning, streets throughout the Reich were littered with broken glass from shattered store windows, from which the night got its eternally famous name – *Kristallnacht.*

The Jews of Lodz began casting uneasy eyes towards their next-door neighbor to the east. Understandably feeling unsafe in their own homes, many began moving away. They were the lucky ones. Because for Lodz the worst was yet to come.

With the German invasion of Poland on September 1, 1939, the Makowskis – like the rest of Poland's 3 million Jews – would see their lives instantly change, becoming persecuted, disenfranchised, marginalized, and eventually murdered by their Nazi occupiers. Marks stands as one of the very few Jewish children from Lodz who survived the forced labor and hunger that would come to characterize Nazi Germany's vast constellation of ghettos and concentration camps.

It was Marks' original intent to publish his memoirs under the title "A Stolen Childhood." However, after realizing how many books by Jewish child survivors there are with this title, he refrained with a heavy heart because with the October 8, 1939 occupation of his hometown through his ultimate liberation on April 29, 1945, he felt his childhood had been stolen. Simply put, at the tender age of seven, Marks had to experience the collective disenfranchisement and deprivation of his family, his neighbors and friends, while also witnessing the murder of the Jews of Lodz.

Marks never knew the carefree feel of going to school, offering both the learning and play that most non-Jewish children his age were able to experience. Instead, in order not to starve, he spent long hours tailoring uniforms for the German Wehrmacht. As an added variable, those inhabiting the ghetto, completely isolated from the outside world, were unsure about their future. While it was true that President of the Government of Kalisch, Friedrich Uebelhoer, had already clearly stated in December 1939 that the ghetto was only a "transitional measure" on the way to an achievable end, the "final goal" was" that we Pestbeule [meaning the Jews] completely burn out. "As it turned out, the disastrous conditions in the ghetto were merely a precursor to something worse as between January 6 and May 15,1942, more than 60,000 men, women and children from the Lodz Ghetto—5,000 Roma among them— were transported to the nearby extermination camp of Chelmno, where tragically they would be gassed.

In 1942, Marks and all the other children under the age of 10 were particularly at risk as, on September 3, news began to spread that the Germans didn't just intend to exterminate the sick and the elderly, but they also wanted to kill all Jewish children younger than 10 years of age. In response, parents tried desperately to hide their children wherever they could while also attempting to modify work documents to make their children appear older than they actually were. When the deportations from September 5- 12, 1942 took place with the transport and extermination of 15,685 sick and elderly along with children under 10 years old at Chelmno, only a few children managed to escape. Marks' parents protected him with false papers, while also hiding his little brother in a number of places so as to foil the Nazis and any potential informants.

This level of security and vigilance within the Makowski family would, during the heavy ghetto years, contribute decisively to Marks' overall will to survive.

With that said, Ber still lived in constant fear of death and, in essence, the peril associated with doing "imaginary work" that he could be punished for, let alone the risk of starvation or perishing at the hands of the many communicable diseases running rampant. In the summer of 1944, the Germans dissolved the ghetto completely with almost all ghetto residents being deported to extermination camps, where most were immediately killed in the gas chambers. Ber narrowly escaped this fate as a slave laborer for the German war industry, this time in the Dachau concentration camp, near Munich. He made it through his will to survive, but especially thanks to the care of his father whose "blessed lie" led the Nazis to believe that his son was older than he actually was. A child of Ber's age was, in the eyes of the Germans, not "fit for work" and therefore had no right to live.

In April 1945 at the mere age of 13, Ber found freedom with the liberation of Europe. Yet the pall of never experiencing a childhood, not to mention the loss of almost all of his relatives, hung heavy. His pre-war home, the Jewish community of Lodz, lay in tatters with only about 5,000 to 7,000 of its original Jewish population surviving.

Today Ber Makowski, now known as Bernard Marks, carries memories of the trauma and terror that his innocent family had to endure. The essence of this book's creation is simple: to personally contribute and carry forth to future generations an understanding of the consequences of a racist and deeply inhumane dictatorship. The book is also a way by which Marks can come face-to-face with the painful memories that linger while, at the same time, embark on a quest for the lost, happy memories of his early childhood in Lodz and his many years as a small boy in the ghetto.

There were obvious reasons not to preserve certain memories; hunger, labor and the prevalence of death meant that the ghetto could be hardly memorable. As historians and those who wish to preserve the historical record, Marks' memories are of special, unique value as they transmit beyond the blandness and business-like official documents of the Nazis. The power of oral history dwells in its ability to convey the individual experiences and feelings of the victims, their shattered lives and worlds, and, of course, their courage and will to survive, all of which is so elegantly brought to current and future generation by Bernard Marks.

This book is based on the formal manuscript of Bernard Marks and the numerous discussions that we had in Landsberg am Lech, Dachau, and during thepast few years in Sacramento, Munich, Uffing am Staffelsee and Landsberg. These meetings always conjured forth special and unique moments. I, therefore, consider it a very great pleasure and honor to be able to both translate his manuscript and write this introduction.

At this point, Bernard Marks and I wish to thank Ursula Vultures of the Dachau Memorial Site (Gedenkstätte KZ-Lager Dachau) in addition to Dr. Michaela Haibl and Peter Koch, who kindly took over the proofreading of the German texts. We would also like to thank the archivist of the Dachau Memorial Site (Gedenkstätte KZ-Lager Dachau) Albert Knoll and to Judith Cohen of the U.S. Holocaust Memorial Museum in Washington, D.C., who supported us generously with research and procurement of photographs. Thanks to all of you for your help.

Barbara Hutzelmann

Chapter 1: My family

I was born in a clinic in Lodz at 2:15 a.m. on September 17, 1932 – the first child born to my parents, Josef Makowski and Laja Pat, who married in Lódz. They named me Ber and I had the distinction of being the first in our family's many generations to not be born at home. An erroneous entry into the birth register recorded my birth year as 1934 and this date followed me as I made my way through my early childhood and enrollment into school. My brother Avram was born three years later – in 1935 - also in Lodz.

My great-grandfather Mortka Makowski and his wife, Sura Zolendz, moved into the Lodz region in the first half of the 19th century. Originally from Gorky, Russia, they settled in Tuszyn, about 20 kilometers south of Lódz. My paternal grandfather, Jakub Mendel, was born in 1868. He had several brothers and sisters, but only one, Froim, is mentioned by name in the old registers. Froim immigrated to the United States in roughly 1882, during the massive wave of emigration that followed the assassination of the Russian Tsar. Jakub Mendel was an ordained rabbi and moved to Lodz, where he would marry my grandmother Bajla Cypa Kuczsynska. Together, they opened an export/import cloth and linen mill. They produced three sons and three daughters: Esther in 1894, Abram Chil in 1897, Sura in 1899, Chaim Majer in 1902, Tauba Fajga in 1904 and Josef in 1906.

All of their children followed in their parents' footsteps, becoming successful entrepreneurs in the textile industry. Uncle Abram later moved to Leipzig, Germany and married Hinda Grodek, who also came from Lodz. Their two children, a son named Moritz and a daughter named Frieda, were born in Leipzig. After Hitler came to power, Uncle Abram visited us in Lodz once. He was already convinced that times would grow to be difficult for us Jews and managed to flee with his family to Argentina.

My grandfather occasionally spoke of the many opportunities that he had to immigrate to America but he preferred to stay in Poland, the land of his birth. He died in 1936 at the age of 68. My father's mother was known in the family as a very rich lady, possessing many large apartment buildings along Zgierska Road – many of them still stand today. Another of her properties, a block away, was demolished after the Second World War to create a municipal park and a monument to the Jews of Hamburg, who had been deported to the Lodz Ghetto during the war.

It's notable that my grandparents never lived in a predominantly Jewish district, but always in a Catholic one on Gdanska Avenue 123. Their address was quite far from both the city center and the Jewish Quarter, but the building – a five-story apartment house – belonged to them, offering their children enough space to live there rent-free. A good thing, it was a Jewish custom for a daughter to marry only after she had her own apartment!

After my father, Joseph, completed twelve years of school, he began to work. He did not want to be a rabbi like his father. He sewed pants and vests for a large supplier and did smaller jobs for individuals for supplementary income. He did all of it with a few Singer sewing machines and irons. On occasion, he would even get orders from the Polish government to produce uniforms. My father was quite enterprising and successful, as early at the age of 15, he enjoyed having a very good reputation for being a skillful uniform tailor.

As the youngest of his siblings, my father was a bit rebellious, not only in how he would choose his career but in his refusal to wear the traditional black Hassidic clothing and yarmulke. At 16, he moved out of his parents' house rented an apartment, and continued his work for major suppliers in the apparel industry.

The maternal side of my family dates back to 1811 in the Polish city of Blaszki, in the province of Kalisz. The family was very involved in educating the Jewish community. My maternal grandfather, Itzchak, was born on June 24, 1873 in Blaszki. Like my paternal grandfather, he was also an ordained rabbi and worked as a teacher in a small yeshiva. He later moved to the larger town of Lodz, drawn by the opportunity to work in a larger Yeshivah, a Religious school.

My mother, Leah (Laja) Pat, a tall blonde with blue eyes, worked for my father as a seamstress. She was the second oldest of six children and was the breadwinner of the family, as my grandfather Itzchak fell seriously ill and could not work any longer. Grandmother Perl Pat was not working outside the home, as far as I know. She kept busy enough with the work of caring for the large family. My mother's oldest sister Sura, who never married, lived at home. The same was probably true for her younger sister Chana as well as her brother Fiszel.

Family Photo - 1938
From left to right: Laja (Mother), Abraham Mordechai (Brother), Ber (Self), Bajla Cypa (Paternal Grandmother), Sura Kalski (Father's sister), Josef (Father)

Paternal Grandmother Bajla Cypa nee Kuszczynska

Maternal Grandmother Perl Pat nee Chaimowicz

Chapter 2: Family life and early childhood memories

I have many memories from my life as a young child before the war. Some relate to family traditions surrounding Sabbath while others are about my experiences at school and learning life lessons from family members.

As the rabbi at a modest synagogue my paternal grandfather, Jakub Menachem Mendel Makowski, was the undisputed head of the family and highly educated in all that concerned the Jewish tradition.

As patriarch of our family, Grandfather Menachem Mendel reached out to me, in a loving way, even contriving practical lessons to keep me interested. He taught me how to make cigarettes when I was just a small child. He used a gadget, which he filled with tobacco, which was then pushed into a pre-filter with a paper sleeve, half tobacco and half filter. Next, he cut the end square with the paper sleeve and laid the final product into a silver box.

Once I wanted to take a burning cigarette from an ashtray which prompted my grandfather to say, "Berele, Dovele" (my Yiddish/Hebrew name) if you want to smoke, I'll give you something really good -- a cigar." He forced me to take a few deep breaths until I turned green. This experience kept me away from smoking until I was 30.

Having a loving paternal Rabbi Menachem Mendel as the head of our family created awareness of our Jewish traditions.

As the weekend was approaching the family went through with a familiar routine.

Thursday's weekly ritual, my father would go on his high speed bicycle to his parent's house to prepare the house for the Sabbath; to scrub the kitchen floor, polish the beautiful wooden floors in the rest of the house wash the windows and bring the groceries for the Sabbath dinner, especially the herring and onions, so grandma could prepare the delicacy chopped herring salad as an appetizer. I can taste it now!

While father was out of the house, I remember my mother, Laja, would start preparing for the Sabbath day "cholent" meal, an East European Jewish delicacy. She took out the black cast iron large pot, placing cubed sections of lean beef, peeled potatoes, vegetables, a stuffed chicken neck consisting of flour, schmaltz (rendered chicken fat), and spices. In the center she placed another smaller pot with carrots, raisins and spices. The main pot was covered, sealed and placed in the basement where it was cold. Friday morning the cast iron pot was taken to a bakery, where it was placed in the ovens for overnight slow simmering using the ovens residual heat. The sweet aroma of the simmering cholent filled our neighborhood.

On Friday afternoon, we started the long walk to my paternal grandparents' house where we always had the Sabbath meal. The house was located at Gdanska

123, in a Christian neighborhood not far from a Polish Army barracks. Grandpa Menachem Mendel purchased a large four-story apartment building to have a place for his three daughters to live once they married.

After the Shabbat evening meal we had to walk through the Christian area of the city to the synagogue located in the Jewish side of town. The residents taunted us with anti-Semitic remarks. The long walk most often was after dark was uncomfortable and dangerous.

The entire family participated in Saturday morning services. The men started early in the morning putting on the *Tefilling* (תפילין) also called *phylacteries* (meaning "to guard, protect") is a set of small black leather boxes containing scrolls of parchment inscribed with verses from the Torah The arm-Tefillin, or *shel yad*, is placed on the upper arm, and the strap wrapped around the arm/hand, hand and fingers; while the head-Tefillin, or *shel rosh*, is placed above the forehead. The Torah commands that they should be worn to serve as a "sign" and "remembrance" that God brought the children of Israel out of Egypt. Then we went to synagogue for the lengthy morning service. It included the prayers and Torah reading and my grandfather, the Rabbi, explained the Torah reading in three languages – Yiddish, Polish and Russian. The members of his congregation spoke these different languages so he made sure everyone could understand. Once the service was over, we shared a small meal as a congregation. During and after the meal, we would discuss the parshah (Torah portion) and everyone would share his or her thoughts about it. At the end, the adults would have a drink of Slivovitz and head home. On the way home my father the strong man would pick up the large cast iron pot from the bakery. The aroma of the hot food was always a delight. We could not wait to open this delicacy. To this day the mere mention of cholent lingers the aroma in my nostrils and the tasting those slowly simmered potatoes, vegetables, and not forgetting the center small pot with the desert food called Tzimis makes my mouth water.

On Saturday afternoon, the second part of the Sabbath celebration, the entire family would walk to my maternal grandparents, Rabbi Itzchak Pat's house. Father would carry the heavy cast iron pot wrapped in many towels to keep the food hot. On the way we went through a beautiful park. It contained an aviary so we could see birds and exotic plants growing in hothouses. I always tried to catch butterflies, which was against the law. When we arrived at my maternal grandparents, the hot meal was served.

At sunset, when Sabbath was over, my grandfather Menachem Mendel would light up a cigarette. Although my grandfather Menachem Mendel was known as a one match man, a chain smoker, he always cautioned others about the harmful effects of smoking. He passed away at the ripe old age of 68 in 1936

Monday was the beginning of the school week. I was one of the few Jewish students enrolled in public school. Many teachers treated us badly because we were

Jews. By the time I entered school, I could already read and write. I was bored and couldn't understand why the other students weren't at my level, so was often disruptive in class. The teachers sat me in the corner, told me to shut up and occasionally hit me on the fingers with a ruler. One teacher, however, was very understanding and allowed me to quickly move from the first to the second and then the third grade.

The same teacher also taught me to be a Polish patriot and appreciate the accomplishments of Tadeusz Kosciuszko. Kosciuszko was educated at the Royal Military Academy. He went to Paris and Dresden because he could not get a job in his native Poland. In 1776, he traveled to Philadelphia and joined the fight for American freedom, eventually becoming a colonel and chief engineer in the Continental Army. In 1783, the U.S. Congress awarded him American citizenship. Later, congress gave him land as a reward for his service with the Continental Army. Upon returning to Poland in 1784 he became involved in the Republican movement. In 1792, he led Polish troops in the Russo-Polish war. Defeated, Kosciuszko fled to Saxony to continue the fight for Polish freedom from Russian domination. Fighting in Prussia in 1794 he was wounded, fell into Russian captivity and was eventually incarcerated in St. Petersburg. After the Tsar pardoned him in 1796, Kosciuszko emigrated again to the United States and later to Switzerland, where he died on October 15, 1817. His body was transferred to Krakow, where he was buried as a Polish patriot and martyr on Wawel Hill.

Another important Polish personality we learned about was Marshal Józef Pilsusdki who became President of Poland. We also learned about Poland's many kings. However, instead of learning the truth – that these same nobles had in fact brought the Jews into the country to promote the economy – it was made known that the Jews had come to Poland to exploit the Christian population. I tried to tell the teacher that the information being taught wasn't correct and she was teaching hate by referring to the Jews as "Parszywy Zyd" which means "dirty Jews".

I had many friends, both Jewish and non-Jewish children with whom I played. I remember Mietek, who enjoyed cutting up into individual frames the movie negatives, which he purchased for a special game. Of course, we also played football (soccer), but the caretaker at the apartment house of my great-aunt Alta Priva constantly took the ball away fearful that we would smash the windows.

Visiting my maternal grandparents was different from my paternal grandparents. They lived in a very large apartment building on the third floor. For some reason the stairwell, was always dark. To walk up so many spiraling wooden steps was at times very frightening because I didn't like the darkness. However on the Sabbath day the stairwell was always brightly lit.

An aunt Golda an older sister of my mother, married, and to moved Kielce, 125 miles to the South-

East from Lodz. To visit her and my cousin I used to take the tram around the corner from our house to the main bus station for a direct bus to Kielce. I shall never forget on one of my weekend anticipated potential journeys, my father took me to the tram station to take the bus to Kielce, he suddenly asked, "where is your suitcase?" Frightened, I looked around but couldn't see that he had hidden the suitcase behind his back. He exclaimed "You cannot go alone any longer on this long journey since you're unable to keep track of your belongings." Needless to say, my weekend plans were never the same

As a youngster I was always very inquisitive in mechanical things, what makes it tick, in Yiddish we have an expression," to find out from where your feet grow"

On one occasion was trying help my father to clean our apartment, suddenly my inquisitiveness, "why don't you ever clean our alarm clock that stand on the fireplace shelf?" One evening my parents had gone to the movies I took the alarm clock apart and washed each part thoroughly. Before I could finish the cleaning, my mother and father returned. All I received was that special look from my father. He didn't punish me, but admonished me. You took it apart; now figure out how to put it back together. After many hours, I managed to assemble most of the various wheels in the proper locations, but had a problem to fitting the hairspring correctly. Father was good to me at that juncture of trying to be an engineer. He fitted the hairspring gently into its place and the clock ran OK.

Another time my parents went to the cinema, they arranged the young aunt Chana (Andzia) to watch us, however, she was more interested in visiting downstairs with one of her admirers, leaving us alone for some time, which enabled us to play fireman, by throwing lit newspapers atop the neighborhood's storage sheds, luckily, the flaming papers extinguished themselves preventing the sheds from being burned down. I also thought it would be fun to try on my mother's high heel shoes. Because I found it difficult to walk or run with them, it angered me so I threw them out the window and into the courtyard. Later on, my mother found them outside and, instead of suspecting me, asked her sister angrily, "Where have you been, anyway" it was your responsibility to watch the children, not to visit with your admirers". Mother gathered up all her shoes and placed them back in the shoeboxes.

Grandmother Bajla Cypa nee Kuczynska with my
grandfather Jakub Mendel

TThe grave of my grandfather Jakub Mendel in 1936
Pictured left to right: Aunt Fela Amzel, Baila Cypa
Makowska (Grandmother), Mother Laja (Leah), Josef
(Father), Uncle Chaim Mayer Makowski, uncle Moishe
Kamuszewicz, Aunt Esther Malka Kamuszewicz, and
Aunt Sura Kalski

Chapter 3: Summer Holiday 1939

The 1939 school year ended in mid-July. I was 7 years old and in grammar school, where I had skipped two grade levels, having taught myself to read at age 2. The summers in Lódz were usually hot and humid. That said, my brothers, mother and I couldn't wait to escape the heat, humidity, dust, noise, and crowds of Lodz and start our annual vacation in the countryside. The cottage, with its three rooms, was a wonderful place, mainly because of the huge lake right outside our porch. I spent most of my time enjoying the pleasant coolness, climbing trees and plundering nearby apple orchards.

With all the fun, we also had to dedicate time to the cheder (religious school) so we brought our Hebrew books. Most of the cottages there were rented to Jews, so learning Hebrew and the Torah came easily. As stated earlier, my father almost never wore a kippah or tzitzi even when we went to the grandparents. On the other hand, my mother kept a kosher kitchen so as to not deprive our more orthodox relatives the joy of eating with us.

Summer guests, especially children, fell under a rigorous set of rules of conduct: 1) Take only what you can eat! 2) Break no branches! 3) Do not jump from branch to branch! 4) Tree houses are forbidden and 5) Above all, there would be no swinging from branch to branch with a rope! Although the region was full of orchards and dirty streets, there were also an abundance of beautiful, white birch trees. The farmers had plowed their fields and planted their crops in perfect, straight rows of vegetables and watermelons. They knew all the families who spent the summer there and most of us traveled to the countryside every year was to relax in the freshly whitewashed summer houses. All the windows were fitted with fly screens to keep out annoying pests.

The renters also had strict regulations throughout the cottage area. Any child not adhering to such rules had to reckon with the corresponding consequences. Parents had to pay for all damages or for any watermelons that were stolen from the fields. Simply put, the affected farmers had to be compensated - and for more than just a fruit. Yet, my brother, Avram, and I could not resist the apples and watermelons. And not just once, we smashed melons by throwing them to the ground until they burst open. I won't deny it – it was a fun sport for us! My father ended up having to compensate the peasants for the damages. As punishment, we were not allowed to read our children books, nor write our summer assignments, and swimming in the lake was forbidden for one day. However, we were forced to write letters of apologies to the farmers for some time. Father could be quite severe. Following the lengthy letters of apologies, we had to resume the summer school assignments late into the night

For our meals, Mother bought most of the food at the many surrounding farms. Something I particularly loved was kefir - a tangy, thick milk with small grains resembling cauliflower. Kefir consisted of equal amounts of fresh and boiled milk and was only stored for a few days in the cool cellar before it could be consumed.

On the weekends, my father would close his factory and cycle with cousins and uncles the 25 to 30 kilometers to us in the country. They could take a tram that connected them to the city's suburbs and smaller villages. My father was an avid sportsman, and biking kept him fit and strong My uncle Fiszel, who rode a motor bike, could barely keep up with my father's pace, he usually would leave his bicycle at the cottage. After the long rides into the country, most of the accompanying cousins and uncles, sweaty faces and all, completely exhausted from the tour. Not surprisingly, and the first thing they did upon arriving at Radogoszcz was jump into the lake to cool off.

Once Uncle Fiszel took me into the forest to show me how to ride his particular racing bicycle, which was called a "Cingel" in Polish. Since I wasn't tall enough to reach the pedals on this adult bike, I was forced to slip beneath the top bar to reach the pedals. Uncle Fiszel simply gave me a big shove from the back. Off I went, confidently steering between the trees until I needed to stop. Then, the inevitable happened. I would just fall on the soft ground under the bike, suffering a few abrasions. When Uncle Fiszel found me, he laughed uproariously at my misfortune but that didn't stop him from teaching me to be a pretty good cyclist.

With our carefree summer vacation coming to an end, I was looking forward to being back in school. The last week of August was quite uneventful, but always with the same daily routine - running in the fields, climbing trees, and, of course, swimming in the lake. I also kept busy collecting butterflies of various colors for a forthcoming school project.

Chapter 4: Last Happy Days

Upon returning to the city after the holidays, there were numerous rumors in circulation – a war with Germany did not seem to be impossible. We heard all these political discussions about the Nazis and that a policy of appeasement to Germany's Adolf Hitler was necessary to avoid war. Being so young, it was hard for me to gauge the importance of it all, but it soon became clear that Poland was Hitler's next target under the flimsy pretext of "reclaiming" the largely ethnic German city of Danzig. Rumors, rumors, rumors everywhere! As a small boy, I was not interested in most of the politics, but do recall asking my father if Danzig was really a German city as Hitler claimed.

The most important thing to me was the upcoming school year. The city of Lodz had adopted specific rules governing public schools. Parents were asked to submit certified copies of birth certificates and the most recent school report for the enrollment of students. My father always complained about these requirements because, of course, the certified copies cost something. In addition, parents had to wait in long lines in the hall at the registry office that issued the birth certificates.

I was eventually provided with proper documentation to attend school, by way of my mother, and able to enroll for the coming school year. I was over the moon with excitement, especially because of my love for math and the desire to leave all of my classmates in the dust. I was really good at it. During those idyllic summer weeks in the country, my mother, insisting that only practice makes perfect, let me solve many problems in math, geography, history, reading, and spelling. My mother had a very good knowledge of geography and history. She drew us maps, for example, of Argentina and Paris, both places where relatives of ours lived. When I was finally enrolled, it was at a school that was relatively close to home, but far enough away that I had to take the tram there every day.

I'll never forget Nowomiejska 34. The three-story building stood at the corner of Nowomiejska and Zydowska streets. As a result, we had two addresses: one for the Christians and one for the Jews. If a Christian asked where I lived, I would say Nowomiejska. If a Jew asked, I would say Zydowska.

We lived on the second floor at Nowomiejska 34. Mr. Goldberg and his family lived above us on the third floor. Mr. Goldberg manufactured caps and his entire apartment was filled with special sewing machines to produce caps. His problem was that he operated an unlicensed factory. To hide it from the authorities, Mr. Goldberg would remove the stairway light bulb leading to this mysterious third floor.

Later, we moved into our newly built modern apartment building located in the Jewish neighborhood, where most of my mother's relatives lived nearby. It had narrow streets and alleyways, dimly lit stairwells, small shops, and many specialty shops. There was one particular shop that I quite liked. Every day after school, I went there and plunged my hand into the cold brine of a huge barrel, extracting a large half-dill pickle. I had to wait for the delivery of the warm, freshly baked Kaiser rolls to enjoy my daily feast. Luckily, the owner made sure the bill wasn't too much of a burden on my parents.

We were now living on the Bazarna 7, in a modern apartment with an indoor toilet and a bathroom with a shower with running water and a flushing toilet. We lived on the third floor, in apartment No. 23. The walls of the bedroom and dining room were adorned with pretty wallpaper, and my parents even bought new furniture. The apartment had been newly painted before we moved in, which fascinated me. First, the workmen would paint the room in a pale blue, and then they would conjure delicate patterns by way of a rubber roller with a pattern. I was so enraptured with the process that I rolled a beautiful design on my own arm when no one was looking. I was eventually found out, which made the painters angry, and my mother had to scrape off the paint immediately. In the bedroom, we had floor to ceiling large white tiled heating furnace with a single shining dainty rose in the center on one of the tiles.

Father installed a dark red security door that had a special locking mechanism. To reach the apartment, you had to turn the key in a specific sequence. Between the two doors, there was a gap where our bikes were suspended. The apartment complex had a courtyard with storage lockers for each apartment unit, but we preferred to keep our bikes in the apartment, attached to the hallway ceiling, so as to keep them from being stolen. After moving into our chic, new apartment, Father made a move to a new textiles factory where he took up a position as a designer for women's and men's clothing.

As the last week of August 1939 was drawing to a close, I began to feel excited for the start of school despite rumors of a war with Germany, which was scary for a boy my age. Sometime in September 1939, I recall running to the main road reaching Freedom Plaza (Platz Wolnoici) to watch the Polish army mobilizing, by horse and wooden wagons, some motorcycles with sidecars and some cavalry units. I eagerly and happily distributed melon slices to our brave soldiers. This filled me with an enormous sense of patriotism.

Little Ber (Bernard)

Chapter 5: The German Invasion of Poland

On the last night of August 1939, we heard the English-operated BBC reporting that troops of the German army were beginning to mass on the Polish border. The next day, September 1, 1939, Radio Lódz announced that a war readiness exercise would take place. Right after the city's air raid sirens were tested, all residents were asked to stay in their homes. With no bombs and no shots, the radio announcer said, "That was an air raid drill," prompting people to return to their daily living activities. That evening, however, Radio Lodz reported that the Germans had invaded Poland and that fierce fighting was raging in the border area. It was clear to us all that the brave Polish Army would repel the aggressor and re-conquer any lost territory. Then it happened: a real air raid alarm was sounded.

In southern Poland, Czenstochowa and Katowice fell, followed by Kraków. It was announced over the radio that all men up to the age of 40 would be needed for general mobilization. In the following days, panic began to spread. Many Poles, including Jews, fled the city. My mother, however, decided to stay, hoping that everything would turn out again for the better. She had already made a similar decision in 1938, namely not to emigrate to Argentina even though we were totally ready to go with our visas, travel documents, and passports. There also had been negotiations underway for the sale of our apartment, furnishings and other household items. In the end, Mother just couldn't be separated from her family – brothers, sisters, father and mother. As she would say, "This is our home, our country." So we stayed. She was a strong-willed woman as well as tall and blond, who could have easily been mistaken for a Christian. My brother Avram was also blond and blue-eyed, but very small for his age. He suffered from chronic colds and asthma and was allergic to many foods, especially meat and poultry products. Perhaps Mother's decision to stay was in part to preclude the long, arduous trip for her fragile young son.

During the rest of the first week of September 1939, the panic continued. People left the city, but only toward the east, to Russia , as that was the only realistic escape route. We heard that the fighting on the front was fierce with the glorious Polish Army repulsing the Wehrmacht at every turn. That didn't last very long.

On September 8, 1939, the Germans marched into Lodz, some on horseback, but many with trucks, motorcycles with sidecars, and tanks. The Germans were welcomed by the local Volksdeutsche or ethnic Germans enthusiastically raising their arms with „Zieg Heil" and throwing flowers. The people on the main street, Piotrkowska, seemed to be overjoyed. I was amazed at how many people welcomed the Germans!

The first day of the German occupation was chaos. On the second and third days, I was astonished to find that the City Hall workers had changed all the street names. The main street was changed to Adolf Hitler Strasse, the next to Hermann Göring Straße. Adding insult to injury, the main junction, with the large roundabout and the monument of our hero, General

Kosciuszko, was immediately renamed Freedom Plaza to Freiheit Platz. As a young boy, I could not understand why – Kosciuszko what was the reason, what had he done to them the Germans. I learned later, this was one way of many that the Germans would try to suppress the Polish spirit.

A few days later, all hell broke loose. The Germans immediately unleashed an unprecedented terror against the Jewish population, and our own citizens, the ethnic Germans enjoyed their freshly harvested power. Stealing, looting and beatings were commonplace.In the city center, all Jews were expelled from their homes and their property was confiscated. German soldiers handled Jews by force, beating them and driving them from their jobs. Jews also suffered the humiliation of being ordered to undress and face a wall. Although shots were fired, no one was killed.

On September 13, 1939 it was time for Rosh Hashanah, the Jewish New Year. However, all the synagogues were closed in Lodz, in addition to being monitored by the SS and the German military. The rest of September was equally bad as Jews were beaten by German soldiers and stores owned by Jews were looted including my Aunt Chanah's (Andzia's) high-end clothing store. Raids such as these were a constant threat for the Jewish population. In order to stop such discriminatory behavior and stop the work stoppages, for this purpose, the Board of Jewish Community agreed with the German occupiers to provide 600 young men on a daily basis to perform menial humiliating tasks.

In September, the German Military Government prohibited the Jews from the production of textiles, leather and clothing. As a result of this, my father's factory was closed and confiscated the machinery was moved out. Later on, these sewing machines, pressing irons, cloth cutting tables and the like were used in production of clothing in the ghetto factories where Jews worked as slave laborers. German officers and local police also continued the confiscation of radios and other household goods. They came to our apartment and took away all of our gold rings, diamonds and anything of any value with the exception of the furniture.

On 13 October, 1939, Albert Leister, the German commander of Lodz, wanted to know who was the President of the Jewish Council. Chaim Rumkowski misunderstood the word for "President" since it is similar to the German word for "eldest." He raised his hand and was thusly appointed by Leister as President of the Judenrat (Jewish Council).

An order issued by the commissioner of Łódź to the management of the Jewish Congregation of Łódź on October 5, 1939. The Jewish Congregation was obliged to provide 700 men daily for work.

On November 7, 1939, it was declared in the Lodz' German-language newspaper that the annexation of Lodz and western Poland was now part of the "Third Reich." What's more, Jews were prohibited from using the city's main road Piotrkowska, now Adolf Hitler Strasse. The occupying forces also ordered all Jews to wear a yellow star to be worn on their clothing and for all Jewish businesses to be labeled with a sign in German as "Jewish-owned."

Atrocities against the city's Jews did not stop, continuing well into November. Many anti-Jewish acts were now being committed by the newly formed Nazi youth organization. They held parades, marched and sang German songs. Time and again, Jews were arrested in raids and forced to do humiliating work in and around the city.

On November 10, 1939, as a warning to the Polish people, and especially the Jews, three people – two Poles and one Jew were hanged in Baluty Market for alleged criminal offenses against the Reich. I didn't see this. However, around this time, at my tender, young age, I witnessed an equally gruesome affair while visiting my father at his workplace.

The Germans were readying to dynamite one of the city's magnificent monuments, a man shouted from a window on the top floor of a nearby building that they not destroy this magnificent monument of Koszczusko. Whether he was pushed or jumped to his death is still a mystery to me. Either way, the sight of a man with a crushed skull on the sidewalk will for be etched into my memory.

On November 17, 1939, I was out on the town. On this glorious autumn day, the German SS blew up the statue of General Tadeusz Kosciuszko, the great Polish patriot and national hero, on the Wolnosci Plaza (Peace Plaza). In the midst of the following silence and shock that most of us felt, I realized that the thunderous explosion extinguished so much of the inner peace that had characterized my childhood years. Nestled deep into my memory was the fact that the marauding Nazis, after invading our lives, had realized their crowning achievement: blowing up the memorial of our beloved folk hero. Yet, even after the detonation had died away, it was clear that although the statue had toppled, it was far from broken. The chiseled chin and strong shoulders were all recognizable, as if he were ready to gallop on horseback from village to village, summoning Poland to resist the Teutons.

I had discovered that my friend, Chaim, was also in the crowd. He ran over to me and we headed home together. On the way, we were stopped by a large gang of crooks in trucks, packed with sledgehammers. They surrounded us from all sides and forced us back towards the destroyed statue. One of them laughed, throwing a hammer down on the street right in front of our feet while their leader shouted through a megaphone, "Come on, you fools finish it here! Make lots of Dust! Dust is all that will be left before you leave from here! "

Stunned and frightened, Chaim and I looked at each other and waited for a sign from someone, from anyone, as to what to do next. Then, in an effort to extract ourselves from the situation, we began slowly to move toward the park. Again, we were immediately surrounded. One of the gangsters handed us hammers and their leader shouted, "Go, go! You will make the first blow, or we'll do it!" I knew what we had to do. Sledgehammers would be in action all day. Each of us took one of these tools and slowly began to swing them through the air, crushing the statue into dust as they commanded. The leader stood on one of the trucks, roaring with laughter as we carried out his desired destruction.

A few days after the loss of the statue, the largest and oldest reform synagogue, located on Kosciuszko Boulevard, was blown up and burned to the ground. The Jewish community was forced to look at all of this, making it clear that we were becoming less and less the masters of our own destiny. The German army demanded 25 million zloty in exchange for the termination of terror against the Jewish population. Since this wasn't possible, the cruel harassment continued unhindered. German soldiers and SS officers ransacked endlessly all the Jewish apartments on the main street, and randomly remove furniture, they even took clothing, food, art objects and on and on. A deeply humiliating insult was the imposition of a curfew, starting on the 15th of September Jews were forced to stay in their homes between 5:00 p.m. and

7:00 am. This was followed by the disturbing news that many Jews would soon be deported to special labor camps outside of Lodz.

In mid-December 1939, the entire central part of the city was "cleansed" of any Jewish presence by the submissive cooperation of city leaders with their German overlords. The deportations from Lodz to different parts of the newly formed Reichsgau Warrtheland (annexed part of Poland to Germany) were now in full swing with thousands of teachers, doctors, engineers, and their families finding their way into bondage. No one actually knew why.

The German invasion of Lodz. Pictured in the background is the monument of the national hero of Poland, General Tadeusz Kosciuszko, on Freedom Plaza.

Chapter 6: Ghetto

By January 1940, the first rumors came out that all Jews would have to move into a ghetto. By February 8, however, we were informed by the police that it wasn't a rumor anymore, but actually true.

On February 12, 1940, the Germans began to round up the Jewish population of Lodz like cattle, guiding them into the Baluty and Maryszin Quarters. Our new apartment at Bazarna Square fell within these collective zones, but all the Jews who lived outside of the district were now forced to move there, leaving the homes they knew and being allowed to bring very little of their possessions. It was at this point that we saw something completely new to us: German soldiers taking just what they wanted from the packed carts of Jewish families and simply driving away.

At the beginning of 1940, the newly appointed German police chief ordered all non-Jews to avoid the "Jewish District" because of the risk of infectious diseases supposedly emanating from us Jews. This was a typical Nazi lie or superstition regarding Poland's Jews. Despite that, we tried to adjust to life in the Baluty slum area, which lacked the modern niceties that we were used too. Even more demoralizing was the unkind scale of the area as it covered a mere four and a half square kilometers for a total of 160,000 Jews! About 30 percent of the Lodz population was comprised of Jews. Not surprisingly, having space in the ghetto became a privilege as the number of available spaces decreased daily with more and more people pouring into Baluty.

This truly hit home as the Jewish Council sent two brothers to occupy our kitchen our modest-sized apartment.

Making a difficult situation even more challenging, our living room was given to a family of three, while we were now relegated to living in both bedrooms. A total of nine people shared a kitchen, bathroom and toilet. The best we could do was devise a schedule for the specific use of each space, in the hopes of producing some semblance of normalcy. And, yet, people still came, including a young couple who occupied a portion of the kitchen. Because they were very much in love with each other, my father—in order to give them some privacy—decided to separate one part of the kitchen from the other with a cloth. My maternal grandfather Itzchak Pat moved in with us for a short period, but passed away December 1939. By the end of 1941, there were about 20 people in our little apartment.

The confined quarters were probably most difficult for the adults with the constant coming and going and the appalling narrowness of everything. Simply put, with only a few toilets, and no sewage system, darkened streets, and no street lights, life was becoming harder and harder by the day. Adding insult to injury, the Germans were merciless, confiscating everything and forcing old or middle aged people to sweep the streets or perform other work which they had never done before. At first, we were allowed to leave Baluty and go to town. Later, however, in April 1940, that changed. Barbed wire fences surrounded the Jewish residential district, patrolled by German soldiers with German Shepherds. By April 30, 1940 the ghetto was closed and, on May 10, finally and completely the Jews were sealed off from the rest of the city.

Months later, we suddenly saw new police forces. It occurred to us that they were from Germany, as their helmets indicated; they were units of the Hamburg police to be exact. They now began to behave as masters over us, giving birth to a new wave of violence. It was through a child's eyes – my eyes – that I saw something terribly brutal and completely outside my realm of understanding. Our exact location in Baluty was near the Bazaar Square. It was there that the Germans constructed a massive gallows. 40 Jews, some of whom I knew, were brought to this place. They were doctors, lawyers, journalists, musicians - all intellectuals - and some were even my teachers. All of us, numbering in the thousands, were forced to watch their collective execution. A high-ranking SS officer gave a short speech, assuring us that "This [was] not the first and not the last execution. It shall be to you Jews a lesson that the laws of the 'Third Reich' must be complied. The smallest level of disobedience to these laws and you're next."

I'll never forget how the executioner approached the victims, placing loops of heavy rope around their necks. He then examined the noose on a woman, seemingly wondering if the rope was strong enough. After a short while, a board was dropped from beneath the feet, freeing all 40 of them into the void. It was a slow, painful death and we had to watch to the end. All told, we were there about two to three hours. They were left hanging through the day and night, next day, they were loaded onto trucks and taken to the large cemetery in the district of Maryszin. It was nearly impossible for me to process what I had just seen. What had these 40 intellectual people done? I asked questions, but got no responses, it just did not make any sense. The gallows stood for months. Additional executions took place in 1940 and 1941.

The Commissioner of what was now called Lodz City, the mayor, the district president of Kalisch, the Gestapo, the SS and many other German authorities had all made proclamations, rules, and regulations which were affixed to the perimeter of the ghetto. The "Jewish Elder" Chaim Rumkowski was also ordered to establish a Jewish Police Service, to patrol inside the fence to prevent people from leaving the ghetto.

Registration of my family for the "Lodz Ghetto" - 1940

Chapter 7: Life in the ghetto

After the closure of the ghetto, deportations of thousands of Jewish families were continuing to other parts of Poland. The Judenrat (the Jewish Council) however, assured us that life and our living conditions would improve soon. The closure of the ghetto made us a city of our own with our own fire department, police department, post office and other services. It was through this that some measure of normalcy was brought into our daily lives. This was nothing more than an illusion, however, as rationing started and our food allotments dropped significantly. The "Jewish Elder" Chaim Rumkowski, who had been used by the Germans as nothing more than a puppet, did try to ease our lives. Some ghetto inhabitants referred to him as the self-crowned "Melech (King) Rumkowski."

Just as Jews were transported out from the ghetto, the Germans transported new groups of Jews from other parts of Europe into the ghetto. One of the first groups appeared to have come in on a first class train from Berlin. Others came from Hamburg, Frankfurt, Cologne, Vienna, Prague and many other places. The ladies were magnificently dressed, with exquisite dresses and hats. Along with their copious amounts of baggage, the kids had rosy cheeks and the men wore handsome overcoats, gloves and hats. It was obvious that they were not poor in their former homeland.

Then came a new transport consisting of thousands of "Gypsies," known also as Romani. They were fenced into a special part of the ghetto. We weren't allowed to go near the Romani section, nor can I ever remember having seen them outside of their assigned homes. At this time, the SS took over the complete surveillance and control of the gypsy camp. Some months later most Romani were dead; so many thousands of people killed just because they were Gypsies!

There was also a church in the ghetto area: the Church of the Blessed Virgin Mary. In this building, the Gestapo set up its headquarters where they dragged people in to be interrogated and beaten, supported by the newly empowered ethnic Germans. The Volksdeutsche (Poles of German ancestry) accounted for approximately 60 percent of the Christian population of the city, and they were clearly on the side of the Nazis. Most of them also spoke Yiddish, for they worked for Jews and had friends and neighbors who were Jewish. They also knew who had money or gold, and who was a factory owner which means they knew practically everything about us. They were often informers for the Gestapo, German Criminal Police, the SS and the Wehrmacht. We were constantly being watched by the Jewish police on one side of the fence and the Wehrmacht police on the other.

Despite the constant surveillance, some brave folks managed to slip through the barbed wire to buy food from the Poles. Part of what became a flourishing black market with prices going sky-high by the day. And although the German attacks became fewer and fewer, murders occurred daily along the fence line. The Guards, consisted mainly of former German officers, who were not Wehrmacht members. People were simply shot, most of the time for no particular reason, or perhaps because they had gotten a little too close to the barbed wire fence, or because they decided to have a brief conversation with a friend who now lived on the Christian side.

One particular incident involved an ethnic German who lived in the Zelony Rynek (Green Market) district of Lodz. His name was Janek and he went by the nickname Red Head. He sold a considerable amount of food on the black market. Together, he and a former boss named Alyezer operated what was now a lively trade, especially with chickens and eggs. Things went very badly after the Jewish police confiscated some 25 hens, leaving Janek without any payment. Janek told Alyezer that he would kill a Jew for any unpaid hen. Over the next three weeks, he shot and killed 35 Jews while the German police stood by and watched. Janek was the most disgusting creature outside the ghetto.

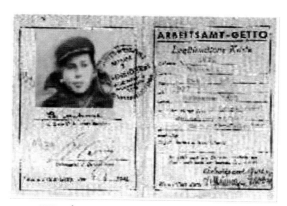

Work permit of Ber Makowski

Chapter 8: Slave Labor

Hans Biebow was a hard luck entrepreneur who, prior to the war, hadn't done much in Germany. He did know, however, how to leverage Jewish labor for the benefit of both himself and the Third Reich. Biebow suggested the establishment in the ghetto of labor departments for tailors, shoemakers, furniture joiners, straw shoe manufacturers and much more. The German government approved the plan and appointed Biebow head; as such, he could do what he wanted. Biebow convinced German companies to make use of the labor in the Lodz Ghetto, inviting German entrepreneurs, including high-ranking Nazi officials, to see the caliber of uniforms, shoes, furniture and dresses that were being manufactured. He even organized a fashion show where women's dresses, suits, coats, men's clothing and embroidery (including rank insignia) could be shown off. From Germany, he received orders for jackets, trousers, coats or shoes. We worked, he earned money, and, in return, we received ration cards with which we could purchase bread, soup or milk. In order to get milk, you had to go to a doctor and obtain a prescription. When you received this prescription, your work permit was confiscated and you were identified as being sick and then sent out of the ghetto. We later learned these individuals were sent to a extermination camp called Chelmno.

It was near my birthday when my father had to register me as a cloth cutter. Because I was to work with him, I was given a work permit which enabled me to receive a ration card. This was vital to be able to buy rations. I worked as a young boy with my father, who had made me five years older than my actual age, and was one of the youngest workers in the ghetto with a permit. In 1940, I only worked a few hours a day in order not to lose my working card. After 1941, however, I worked all day like everyone else. Factories emerged in virtually every craft, making the ghetto a beehive of production for the Nazi regime. The bitter truth of it was that we had to eat which meant that we traded our labor for food.

I toiled ten hours a day, which entitled me the merit of five "scripts." After work, I ran to buy my fill but as I stood at the end of the distribution line, I came to realize that I never really had money per se, because the "scripts" were simply for food and nothing else.

Manufacturing straw overshoes

In the furniture factory

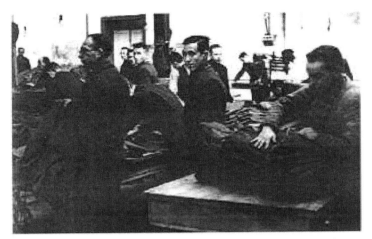

In the tailor shop – at the right background is the
cloth cutting machine (band saw)

1943

Photo from the Berlin Archives, 1943.
Ber (Bernard) directly behind and left of man with star

Chapter 9: Survival

Life in the ghetto from May to August 1940 got worse and worse. Because food rations in the ghetto were so low, it was common to see the corpses of those who had starved lying in the streets. We all just tried to rise above it. Ten to fifteen carts were designated to come through the streets and gather up corpses for transportation to the cemetery. This was hard to see, but I possessed a strong will to live.

We weren't sure what was happening in other places, but it was exceedingly clear to us that children under 10 years old were being taken away from the ghetto. We later learned that they were taken to the extermination camp at Chelmno where they were all gassed. There were no gas chambers; rather, they were sealed into and driven in a converted ambulance until they died from carbon monoxide poisoning. My little brother Avram was so much younger than me, but we luckily managed to hide him in the ghetto.

Every time the Germans or the Jewish police made their raids, we succeeded in moving Avram to another location, sometimes hiding him under clothes in my father's factory. In hospitals, the Jewish and German police would take children under 10 and throw them out of the window onto trucks. We hid my little brother anywhere to protect him. He was so small he could hide in drawers, in cupboards -- sometimes my mother and father even wrapped him in a blanket and took him to work so he was never home alone.

The Germans closed the ghetto's schools in October 1941. In the evening, however, I went to a secret school, a cheder, (a Jewish school) where we were taught not only religion but geography, Polish grammar, Hebrew, Jewish history and, once in a while, Russian. This school was located on the first floor of Lagiewnicka Street number 8. This was the residence of my maternal grandfather, Itzchak Pat, a rabbi. He was ill by this time but had trained other rabbis, one of which was teaching us at this secret school. There were 10 to 15 of us that learned in an environment consisting of a few tables and chairs. Our teacher was a well-educated man in his mid-30s who was a student of my grandfather. Lessons were prepared in small notebooks because the Germans had seized all of our textbooks.

And, of course, we just wanted to play as all children do. Sometimes we played football (soccer). We would also purchase foot-long film strips for about two pennies and cut them into individual frames. Each of us would take a turn flipping our film strip on the staircase. If yours landed on someone else's, you would win their film strip. The object of the game was to win as many strips as you could. The one with the most strips at the end could go into the store and redeem his film strips for a Kaiser roll and a pickle. Girls weren't permitted to join us in this game. They had a similar game just for girls where they used paper rolled into small balls and flipped those across a chalk line. The furthest ball from the chalk line was the winner.

I had some friends. On the one hand, I worked all day and, on the other, I was just a frightened little boy. When a child would laugh or threaten me, I would quickly run to my father. However, my brother, Avram, always fought back when he was provoked or attacked. I preferred to read – for me, that was the most beautiful pastime. In the secret school, I befriended an older boy named David Osowski. We worked in the tailoring shops together and always sat next to each other for our lunch break in the factory courtyard. I recall having two other friends in the ghetto: Meir, who had come from Germany, and Boris, who was from Czechoslovakia. Neither spoke Yiddish or Polish as I did and I spoke no German. I did know a little Czech because of its linguistic relationship to Polish. Over time, they both learned a little Yiddish. Unfortunately, I later lost touch with both Meir and Boris and don't know if they managed to survive.

Sometimes, mother, father, Avram and I would visit my grandmother who, at one time, was a very wealthy woman. She owned no less than four apartment buildings in the current ghetto area. When she died in 1942, my father's niece Sura Tauba ran into the factory to fetch him. He managed to get a permit to go outside the ghetto to go the town hall and had his mother's death recorded and notarized. This enabled my father to avoid having my grandmother buried in the ghetto cemetery, but instead buried in the old Jewish small Jewish cemetery in Lodz.

It was with increasing frequency that I visited my maternal great aunt, Aunt Alta Priva. Her family owned a yarn spinning factory and were very successful. She told some of the most outrageous adventure stories, such as how she had once been arrested in Russia by the Tzarist police. At the time, I considered this to be nothing more than the fictions of an old woman. It was only years after the war, while researching my family history in Russian archive documents to produce a family tree that I found to my great astonishment that all of the stories she told were true.

I located a great amount of family documentation in the Lodz 100-year archives written in Russian as well as documentation in Polish. With the assistance of the archivist, we located the passport of my Great Aunt Alta Prava. Inside, it noted that her passport was confiscated because she was caught in a non-Jewish area where she wasn't allowed to be. I also discovered that one of her daughters died of mental illness at the age of 20. In these same archives, I even located all of the original documents my father completed to apply for immigration to Argentina and found that my maternal grandfather's family originally came from Gorky, Russia and then settled in Tuszyn, about 20 kilometers from Lodz. My grandfather Menachem Mendel was born in Tuszyn in 1868 and became the first ordained rabbi in Lodz.

As a result of these initial findings, I returned to Poland and was able to purchase copies of birth, marriage and death certificates of all my relatives from both sides of my family, as well as my own public school registration form , including very informative documents regarding visas for Argentina documents. I then visited the Jewish cemetery in Lodz and located the gravesite of Menachem Mendel, my paternal grandfather, including the damaged headstone. I found pieces of the headstone and half of the nameplate and was able to reconstruct it piece by piece by referencing the family photo at his gravesite from 1936. I had a new marble nameplate made and returned to Poland to place it on his headstone with the help of the Christian caretaker who was a friend of our family. This same caretaker had saved the Torah scrolls from burning when the Germans set fire to my grandfather's wooden synagogue. He hid one in the walls of his own residence and one in Radon, Poland and one made it to a convent in Zelonka, Poland where it is used today as an educational tool. I was able to find and bring two of them back to Sacramento, where one is used for services and the burned one is on display at Congregation B'nai Israel.

SS officers burning the Torah (private photo)

Chapter 10: Father's arrest

As I mentioned earlier, we lived in a fairly modern apartment which was built just before the war, with a kitchen and flush toilet. At that time, flush toilets were not commonly found in apartments. On evening in mid-1942, there was a sudden hammering on the door. Members of the Jewish police came to the apartment, tearing my father away from my screaming mother. I was astonished and embarrassed, as I had never seen my mother naked. My father wanted to know the reason for the incursion but they said only that he should get dressed, and away they went. My mother was terribly frightened, thinking this might have something to do with Avram, but she soon calmed herself. Father was taken to the Criminal Investigation Department in the Catholic Church of the Blessed Virgin Mary. It was there that they interrogated him and beat him, again and again, for almost a week, in order to tell them where he had hidden foreign currency (dollar and British pounds), gold, diamonds and jewelry.

Meanwhile, mother frantically ran to the German Ghetto authorities to secure his release. She assured both the SS and Gestapo that we possessed no more valuables, as the Gestapo had already confiscated them. Ultimately, Hans Biebow intervened and father was released. I could hardly recognize him. His face was black and blue, his eyes were swollen shut, he had a broken nose and his body was covered with wounds. Fortunately, the police never questioned him about a hidden radio, because, in fact, we had one hidden in our large stove under the tiles of the water container. Father had pulled it out from time to time to listen to the BBC. Thankfully, my father's wounds healed quickly and Biebow was glad to have him back as a worker. This is largely because father saved large amounts of material when laying out the patterns on top of the cloths prior to the cutting.

Today, when I think back to the time my father had to spend in the hands of the criminal investigators, I often wonder how he managed to survive. Was it his will to live? It is well known that only a few of those who entered the church's dungeons ever survived. Was it his strength and athleticism? Father was a former member of the Polish Olympic Team who trained regularly on the rings and was constantly proving his strength. I remember a time when he lifted two sewing machines, each with a weight of 25 to 35 kilos, over his head. He grabbed each sewing machine with one hand, wrapped his palm around the circular parts of the machine, and lifted them at the same time in a position that resembled the outstretched wings of an eagle. Then he raised them slowly over his head and then calmly lowered his outstretched arms back to the floor. He was a member of the Jewish sports club, "Maccabi," where he became versed in any number of sports. And before the war, we lived in a Christian neighborhood quite a distance away from our textile factory, so Father always rode his bike which added to his strength.

Of course, this whole ordeal raised another question. Who was the person who gave the detectives the idea that we possessed such hidden wealth? Was it just an informant who hoped for some reward? Or had it been someone acting out of jealousy because father had a slightly better position and was respected by the Germans?

Chapter 11: Hunger

Even for an adaptable kid like me, it was obvious that the living conditions in the ghetto were getting worse and worse. The winters were terrible and the coal, essential for heating, was nearly non-existent. Food rations were also greatly reduced and the distribution of special rations almost completely stopped. As a result, people in the ghetto were dying. They starved, froze to death, died of disease, or simply opted to commit suicide. On the black market, prices increased immeasurably. Ghetto inhabitants sold furniture or whatever else they had to raise money for additional food.

Rumors began circulating that the Jewish Elder, Chaim Rumkowski, would secure special rations for Rosh Hashanah. Immediately after the new rations were announced, people ran to the distribution center where they fought for a place in the queue when it was their turn to be served , Finding little to no flour, and were only able to snag a few potatoes and some rye flakes.

Food distribution began every Monday morning at 7:00 People scrambled to get everything they could. The hunger in the Ghetto was horrific. A loaf of bread, maybe one pound in weight, was sold for 289 quittung (like Monopoly money). The aptly named "Workshop Soup" cost 12 to 15 quittung. We called this Ghetto money "Rumkies," named after Chaim Rumkowski.

Food was payment for the slave labor rendered in the various factories. The uniforms, jackets and straw shoes that we stitched or manufactured brought in tremendous profits for Hans Biebow.

In order to secure more food, Father started to create things that were needed on the black market. However, a wartime price of a loaf of bread could be inflated a hundred times. Father stole material for gloves and caps from the factory, but he also exchanged such items for food such as potatoes or turnips. Once he was even able to obtain coffee. My mother tried to make pancakes, but they were completely inedible. By the end of 1943, we had almost nothing to eat – only water and horse-grade oatmeal. We have been starving for many days because even with our ration cards, we lacked the money and resources to pay for allotments. My aunt Channah (Andzia) could sometimes get us honey. She showed great skill at smuggling food into the ghetto. Once she even brought us fish oil, not to mention a big block of chocolate. We were allowed to eat a tiny piece of it every day, and it became more precious than gold for us. In time, she no longer visited because she married a butcher. She survived the death march from Auschwitz, and I was able to find her once the war ended at a DP camp in Ansbach, Germany.

Announcement No. 70: Creation of Ghetto money called Quittungen

Ghetto Money (Rumkies)

Chapter 12: The end of the Lodz Ghetto

In June 1944, the Gestapo ordered the liquidation of the Lodz ghetto. Hans Biebow came to our factory in Lagiewnicka Street 45, where I worked as a cutter, and stood on the wooden box next to my machine. He urged us to volunteer for relocation to Germany and promised that all the factories and the machines would be moved into the interior of Germany. I remember him telling us, "It's for your own good. I'll save you from the Russians. It's in Germany that you'll produce for the defense industry of the Third Reich, and you'll help to kill all the Russians."

A fuller speech by Biebow came on August 7, 1944 at 4:45 p.m., after a few introductory words from Rumkowski:

"Ghetto workers! I have talked to you once before and hope that you have taken to heart what I said. The situation in Lodz has continued to deteriorate. All ethnic Germans have been evacuated. Those who believe that the Ghetto is not affected are mistaken. All, without exception, must get away from here. Bombs have fallen within the vicinity of Lodz. The liquidation of the ghetto must be well organized with you going quietly and neatly with me. Factory sections I and II must be taken to safety. Refusing to do so would be hopeless and, as a consequence, we will force you to go if necessary. Four and a half years of cooperation and a unified effort to accomplish excellent work would be destroyed. I give you my word that I'll try anything to get you to safety.

In this war, in which Germany is fighting for his survival, we need workers. Because thousands of Germans have been sent to the Eastern Front on Hitler's orders, Germany is becoming more and more desperate for labor. You would be replacement workers. Our machines are now silent and there is no longer any work going on at the central prison. I sincerely urge you, with the whole staff of factory sections I and II, to report to the train station.

If, however, you'd rather leave for Germany on a later cutter operation, there will be no objection. According to the Council of Elders, this would involve a thousand people, along with their family members, for a total of 2000. For example, a woman who works in the tailor factory and her husband who works in a tapestry (carpet factory) may go together. In all cases, families can stay together and go to camps that are built for this purpose. It is there that factories such as this one will be built. Siemens, A. G. Union Schuckert, and other defense contractors are desperate for labor. In Częstochowa, people are already back to work and very satisfied. After all, you simply want to survive and eat. I hope I have made myself clear. Should you not heed the call, we would simply use force, and this does not rule out the possibility of death or injury. The trip will take about 10 to 16 hours. You will be allowed to take twenty kilos of luggage. It will be ensured that there is enough to eat on the trains. Carelessness and sloppiness will not be tolerated. If you are not reasonable, the ghetto administration will be forced to take more stringent measures. Therefore, I ask you to follow my words – I have nothing further to add.

You'll be paid in Reichsmarks. The managers in the camps are to be Germans. It's to the foreman and instructor that you should report. Come back tomorrow after 12 o'clock to the central prison in the cutter road or to the other collection points. There is enough room for all of you as sufficient wagons and locomotives have been made available.

Please make sure your families bring cooking and eating utensils. These have become scarce in Germany because of their distribution to the victims of the air raids. I will assure you once more that everything else you will need has been taken care of. I implore you to pack your things and sign up. If you so choose to not listen to my appeal, my hands are tied and I can not do anything for you."

The daily transport would each include up to 5,000 people. Only electrically operated equipment was to be taken with hand and foot-operated machines being left behind. The other tailor shops would be closed on Friday and Saturday and, with a break on Sunday, the metal processing plants would be closed on Monday and all machinery and equipment related to the factories would be sent to the mainland of Germany.

Biebow was to submit an evacuation plan. At 7:30 in the morning, a statement arrived, signed by Rumkowski and stating that the main tailoring operation would be evacuated on Thursday. However, Rumkowski's message seemed out of place. It contained no threats or punishment in the event that someone failed to comply. Nor did it mention any action by the Germans if nobody volunteered for the evacuation. The foreman pondered the statement, and came to the conclusion that it must have come from Biebow and his German business associates, none of whom were willing to lose their plants and subsequent profit margins. The sewing foreman estimated that roughly 100 wagons would have to be provided within a few days, but that would only be enough for the workers and their families, without the machinery and other goods. Biebow stated, "Unfortunately, we can't provide you with first-class accommodations so you will be traveling by boxcars. Midway through your journey, we will switch you to first-class trains."

On Wednesday, after finishing soup for lunch, our workshop was asked to prepare a large amount of paper for packing up all the sewing machines in the repair shop.

On Thursday morning, less than a hundred people showed up at the station at Radagoszcz, but they weren't going anywhere due to the lack of trains. Just the day before, Biebow had fervently requested that we all listen to him and be transported to Germany. His voice was made to sound especially sweet when he said, "My Jews." He stated that the evacuation was best for the ghetto's inhabitants because the Eastern Front was moving in our direction and the Russians would punish everyone who worked for the Wehrmacht. His whole speech was free of the harshness that we had grown so accustomed to. For the first time in a long, long time, it seemed that the Jews were feeling some measure of hope.

During lunch, Chaim Rumkowski spoke directly after some of the Ghetto representatives made remarks. He advised people to fall in line with German demands and instructions. Otto Brad Fish, head of the Gestapo in Lodz, spoke next and, with a soft voice, ordered the Jews to voluntarily leave the Ghetto. Biebow again visited some of the specialized workshops and assured everyone that the rulers were driven by a sincere desire to save the Jews from their "self-destruction."

On August 14, 1944, our family was - like so many other ones - transported in sealed cattle cars, each one with 80 to 100 people per wagon. We could only take personal luggage and bedding. Again, we were assured that warm, cozy and pleasant accommodations awaited us at the end of the trip. At the station, our luggage was loaded in separate cars. Nazi assurances sounded something like this, "Do not be afraid, you will get your luggage soon after arrival at the destination! Please pay attention to the fact that your name is clearly written on it!" Before we got on the train we received a large piece of tasty bread, jam, cheese, water and some soup. There were also ostensible plans to load the factory facilities onto flat freight cars with our luggage. We learned later that it was all a ruse. There would be no heavenly relocation to Germany.

In actuality, the wagons were closed and locked from the outside. There was no water and no toilets, and people died during the journey. We resorted to piling the corpses on one side of the car. I do not remember the exact number of dead. The trip lasted two nights and three days, and ended with our arrival in a place called Auschwitz.

August 14, 1944 Transport to the train station in Radagoszcz.
Josef Makowski (circled), Bernard Mark's father

Chapter 13: Arrival at Auschwitz

It was August 16, 1944, and we reached a place without a name – nothing on the station, nothing on the buildings. I noticed that the locomotive, with its steam whistle whining away, approached a huge building where there were twenty or more other freight cars. The train moved very slowly as it passed through the gate of this building. As we made our way through a large gate, the engineer again whistled to indicate the end of the journey. The train stopped so suddenly that it felt like we had been shunted or perhaps hit a type of siding.

The scene was horrific. Peering through the darkness, I could see unshaven, dirty-faced men and unkempt women all beginning to beat on the wooden walls of the wagon. Children gave desperate screams for water. People cursed and kicked each other like wild animals Then we all started to gain a view of the outside environment. It was through a hatch that I saw men in striped uniforms with matching caps. They all looked very healthy and well-fed. Others on the platform, easily identified by their green uniforms, were SS soldiers and officers. They were all carrying rubber truncheons in their hands, some leading about huge German Shepherd dogs.

One of the officers smoked a succession of cigarettes, throwing them on the floor and making a hand gesture in the direction of a large group of armed soldiers. They took guns from their shoulders and fired several volleys into the air. At that moment we heard the metal bars on the outside of the wagon rattle, the doors were flung open, and the masses were unleashed, feverishly grabbing for any fresh air they could find. The troops yelled, "Get back!" The dogs were unleashed on those who did not obey the command. People crowded back after being bitten on the legs and thighs, or kicked by the heavy boots of the German soldiers. Eventually, order was restored.

I could then hear a German SS officer bellow forth a series of new commands: "Leave your luggage and groceries in the car! Carry nothing with you! Those with jewelry, watches, rings, necklaces, gold coins, diamonds or precious stones, foreign exchange and bank notes with them, please pack them back in your suitcase. If you refuse to follow my orders, you will be shot at once!" Some of us felt a desire to fight back, but the men in the striped uniforms advised us to stay the course and avoid being shot or beaten.

Just then, huge military trucks appeared in the distance, slowly approaching the group. The next thing we heard was, "Take off your coats and jackets because you will not need them. You will receive clean coats. Be quick about it and stand on the left hand side!" The men were ordered to one side, women and children on the other. One man asked where we were going, but received no response from the men in the striped suits, most just saying that they understood no Polish or Yiddish. The German officers and soldiers that were present said nothing, and only gave out random commands. Children cried and screamed for their mothers when they were taken from them and thrown into waiting trucks. The old and sick were pushed and shoved into a separate set of trucks and then driven away.

In the distance, we saw high smokestacks. Unwittingly, we could pick up a terrible stench as it wafted through the air. The religious men prayed the "Sh'ma Yisrael, hear us, O Lord!" as they were taken away, never to be seen again. At the infamous ramp at Auschwitz-Birkenau, we were "selected" by Josef Mengele. It was by his momentary gaze – perhaps a fraction of a second – that it was decided who would live and who would die, though we didn't know it at the time. I had to go to the right side of the ramp with my mother and my brother. But my father saw a bit of opportunity and ran to one of the attending SS officers and spoke to him in German.

The officer was amazed that this Polish Jew could speak German so seamlessly. Father said to him, "Look, my son has worked four and a half years in the ghetto already. As stated in his Gestapo papers, he was born in 1927. Leave him with me." Not knowing what would happen, the officer relented, letting me run to my father's side. It was on that very ramp at Auschwitz-Birkenau – August 16, 1944 – that I saw my mother and my brother for the last time.

Those of us now left standing on the ramp had, for the time being, survived and were forced to march about half-an-hour to a large building. Once there, a big, burly man in gray/blue striped pajamas and cap with a red triangle with a number on it on the left side of his jacket spoke to us. He ordered us to undress down to nothing. We were only allowed to keep our belts and shoes. He then told us that rings, watches, gold, diamonds, money and other valuables must be handed over. Failure to comply would result in immediate execution. Father and I weren't hiding anything – it had all already been confiscated. We stood there naked, waiting and waiting. This man so seemed to enjoy his power and punished those who could not stand to attention by beating them with a short stick.

They then forced us to run into a huge hall where another cadre of stripe-clad men examined our bodily orifices for hidden valuables. Those who had gold teeth were brought to yet another location. After the search, they shaved us completely - the entire body from head to armpits and even the pubic hair. They spoke Yiddish, Polish and other languages we did not understand. If that humiliation weren't enough, they then directed us into another hall with shower heads on the ceiling. It was there that we were treated to a short, cold shower with no soap or towels. After that, we were sent outside where we were sprayed with chemicals intended to kill any diseases or vermin we might be carrying with us. We were then ordered to march to another building. There, we were given pants, a long sleeved shirt, and a cap, all in the same gray-blue striped pattern that was so common throughout the camp. No underwear and no socks. Nothing fit. Tall men got small sizes; small men got large sizes. Our group of roughly 500 men and boys began to exchange sizes. It only occurred to me later that excess clothing translated into more warmth. I told myself that next time I would ask for larger-sized clothing. What resonated with me, of all of things that had happened on that day, was the constant running in the nude from building to building.

We were placed in columns like soldiers. They then began to count us, a process that lasted for three hours, all the while standing at attention in the sweltering August heat. Another selection was carried out, during which some of us fainted. Since our departure a few days earlier from the Lodz ghetto we had received neither water nor food. We still had no idea where we were. I asked my father what would happen to us, but he didn't answer. Like so many of us, he, too, was simply fumbling in the dark. He just said, "Do not be afraid, God is watching over us."

At last, someone gave the order to march. No one spoke, no one made a flippant remark. The special prisoners, who we later learned were called "Kapo," would beat anyone who didn't march like a soldier or even whispered. We ran many miles to another camp. Once there, we saw huge barracks, each with the capacity to hold thousands of people.

It was here that the counting began again for hours, in the heat, and without water or food. The Kapos enjoyed beating us, screaming at us, kicking us and making sure that we knew who held sway. At about two o'clock in the morning, after six hours of standing and collapsing, we were directed into a new barracks, one that could accommodate approximately 5,000 people. There were no beds and no bunks, only a bare cement floor. Like sardines, they pressed us in. We were all exhausted and traumatized, and all we wanted was to sleep. However, at 4:30 in the morning, the Kapos started to run through the barracks while beating us with their sticks and yelling, "Sit up, fast, fast! Get out! Out to the courtyard!" In military formation, we had complete rows of five. Lined up like soldiers, we were counted by the Kapos with the final number going to the SS. Then we were herded back to the barracks. After what seemed like an eternity we were able to get some rest. Sometime later in the day they gave us, at last , something that barely passed as a piece of bread and a liquid that was supposed to be coffee.

In the afternoon of the same day, I recall looking beyond the barbed wire fence where there were several women, all naked, with shaven heads. They all looked the same and they all tried to cover their breasts with their hands. For me, still a young boy, I had never seen so many naked women before. Suddenly, I realized that one of them was my aunt Andzia. I called to her and she replied with a nod and a few words I could not understand because of the noise. I asked her if she had seen my mother and my brother. She just shook her head no. Our conversation lasted only a few moments, because the Kapo immediately pushed us apart and warned of the most severe penalties for trying to make contact beyond the fences. He said, "This is not even a warning. The next time I catch someone there, he gets

25 lashes on the bare butt!" That was the last time that I ever saw my aunt.

The Kapos were Aryan criminals, and by fulfilling the orders of the SS, they ensured a way of always staying in the good graces of their SS overlords. Most of the time, however, they were simply worse than the SS. We also met some Jewish Kapos with red or green triangles that were no less vicious than the non-Jews.

We finally learned the name of our concentration camp: Auschwitz-Birkenau. It was here that tens of thousands of people were trapped from all over Europe. We were told that it was a transit camp, where we would wait for our next posting to another concentration or labor camp.

There was nothing to do at Auschwitz-Birkenau but work. The Kapos and the Germans shared the supervision of the camp's work groups, which handled tasks such as hauling stones from one place to another and then back to the starting point. Other jobs were outside the camp. Needless to say, life here was a absolute hell. Exercises such as that on the day of our arrival sequence on the first day – when we were prompted to awaken and assemble – were repeated daily. What's more, to sleep on the bare concrete floor without bed or blanket was almost impossible. The overcrowding was rampant, forcing us to often sleep while sitting on the floor with knees up to our chins. In this way, we managed some sleep and even found some peace. Yet, we always had to be cognizant of our surroundings so as to not fall on one another.

There were fierce battles in the barracks at night because of the inhumane, catastrophic conditions. This often brought friend against friend, and even family members against each other, just to grab one millimeter more of space. Since the Kapos did not tolerate the slightest noise we tried to endure as long as possible. When loud noises and fighting did actually break out, the Kapos went into action, kicking and beating their way through the suffering and brutalizing anyone that got in their way. To the Kapos, it did not matter who was guilty. The ability to act out in sadistic ways were always their primary goal. Amidst all of this, I retreated into dreams - dreaming of the day when I would no longer live in this place or of magnificent palaces akin to what I recall seeing in movies.

Surviving the days in Auschwitz was very hard, but the nights were the most gruesome. I recall wanting to turn my head to the sky and ask, "Why, dear G-d, are you letting this happen?" But then I thought of the courage of my father back at the selection ramp. He had pulled me out of the line where my mother and little Avram stood and, in doing so, placed me on the side of life, as we would later realize. There wasn't a night that went by when someone didn't die from the conditions. We were all so close together, like sardines in a can, with one's head next to the feet of the person next to you. People starved to death, died of thirst, choked, died of disease. Some even found themselves so unable to endure one more day of life under these conditions that they simply ran into the electrified barbed wire surrounding the camp. In the morning, a grim harvest of dead bodies were pulled from the barracks and counted out during morning assembly.

As far as I can remember, we were always given a piece of bread and cup of coffee, but only after counting was done. My father and I were successful, numerous times, in escaping this excruciating five-to-six hour counting and re- counting. The SS was never satisfied with the "number." And once the count was done, the selection for the various work commands began. At approximately two o'clock each day, we received a thin soup - mainly water with lots of sand and salt, in which swam a few potato peelings or a piece of carrot. Without spoons, we drank the soup while standing. We did it quickly as there were usually not enough bowls for everyone. The only thing we had in our possession was our striped uniform - a pair of pants without pockets, a shirt, and a hat.

Father and I stayed at Auschwitz for ten days, all the while under the most appalling conditions. It was common for Auschwitz's prisoners to be tattooed on the forearm with an identifying number, but neither I nor my father had this done. We invented a game: I would ask the SS man if I could go to the latrine and then my father would chase after me. This technique worked well until we were transferred to Dachau.

Transport arriving to Birkenau and selection ramp
(Personal photo)

Chapter 14: Back on transport

It suddenly happened at four in the morning. The Kapos ordered us out of the barracks and into the darkness. Father noticed a truck that was about to leave our area through a gate, away from the barbed wire. At that moment, he whispered to me, "Race to the truck and jump on!" We both managed to get on the truck, thinking it would be our way to freedom. As it turned out, it took us to a train with the already familiar cattle cars. As before, it contained a lot of people pressed in like sardines, more than a 100 in a single wagon, and no food, no water, and no toilet. Deja vu.

Once in place, everyone had to say his or her number or show his or her tattooed arm. Each wagon was supplied with a bucket as a toilet, each was given a piece of bread, and a small ration of water was distributed for sharing. Then the wagons were closed. There was a barbed wire opening only near the top of one side of the cattle car, roughly 50 by 50 inches in area. Because I was small, Father and other adults could pick me up so I could look outside and tell them what I saw. Inside, the cattle car was unbearably hot. No one could sit and it was unbearably tight. After the passing of several hours, the train started to move slowly. We could hear the wheezing and whistling of the locomotive. Between the cattle cars and other wagons, there were SS guards and, at the end of the train, was a flat rail car where German soldiers manned machine guns. I recall asking one of the soldiers why they were so heavily armed. He replied, "You are in protective custody and we have to protect your transport from the Russian bombers." What a grotesque distortion of the facts! Suddenly, the Nazis were playing themselves off as our protectors!

The trip took two days and three nights, during which we were never permitted to leave the wagon. The train stopped several times to pick up people or wait to allow military transports to pass. Through cracks and the aforementioned opening, we deciphered, from time to time, Czechoslovakian place names. The train then turned south going through Austria where, just outside of Linz, it stopped early in the morning for five or six hours. The doors were opened a bit and were able to get some water, but no food. This also gave us a chance to empty the toilet bucket between the tracks under the cattle car.

Our escorts, armed with machine guns, surrounded the entire transport train during the stop. With all these gun barrels set on us, feelings of imminent death started to creep into our collective psyche. I considered the plausibility of father and I tearing one of these weapons away and escaping. The odor inside the hot, filthy, and fetid cattle wagons was indescribable with its stench of urine and excrement. The heat and humidity simply exacerbated the terrible lack of water, food, and medicine. For those who died, all we could do was place them in a corner of the car, piling them up like firewood. The SS guards didn't allow the dead to be carried away, explaining that they needed to provide a record of the same number of prisoners who had been shipped from Auschwitz, dead or alive. The local camp commandant would then be responsible for disposing of the dead. The guards slammed the door shut again, locking it from the outside and off we went. As we did, normal passenger trains with their well-dressed passengers carrying suitcases, ladies adorned with pretty hats, and lots of smartly uniformed soldiers glided into our view.

There were many deaths among the 750 on our transport or, as the SS called it, our relocation for safety reasons. This was nothing more than an additional element to Nazism's so-called "final solution" or the mass extermination of a culture group and faith that I was raised to embrace and love. Because I lived in the Lodz Ghetto from 1940 until August of 1944, I was already familiar with the SS's system of slave labor, deliberate starvation and pre-meditated denial of medical treatment, not even a single aspirin.

After the train passed through Linz, Austria, we seemed to slow down. Taking on more speed, we eventually came into Salzburg where we stopped for about an hour, but this time the doors remained closed. Not surprisingly, more and more people died in our cattle car. Twenty people were already dead, stacked in the corner like a cord of wood. Eighty of us in our wagon were still alive, but barely. Many decided that life simply wasn't worth living, especially the elderly who prayed quietly and had already lost the will to live. In contrast, when we peered out of the train, we would see lovely forests and beautiful fields, cultivated farms and many cows and an abundance of horses. Occasionally, we even saw people. What a juxtaposition!

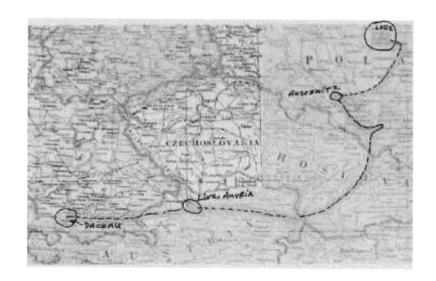

Bernard's (Ber) family transport route from Lodz to
Auschwitz and to Dachau

Chapter 15: From Dachau to Kaufering

At long last, the train arrived at a place we figured to be our destination. One of the guards, an ethnic German from Posen, was constantly happy. Every time the train stopped, he stalked his way by the cattle cars calling out in Polish and sometimes in Yiddish, "If you think life in the ghetto was hard, or survival in Auschwitz was the worse it could get, then just wait for the next place. Consider it your gravesite. All of you Jews will soon be over with, and the world a better place without you in it! You are pigs, stinking pigs, in addition to being subhuman!" He just never mentioned where we were going.

By the third day we reached Munich, Germany where the train needed servicing. The German guards told us that they would end up protecting us and we would eventually arrive at Dachau or another labor camp. It was five-o'clock in the afternoon when the train stopped outside Dachau, which was but a short distance from Munich. We had no idea what awaited us. We had, in effect, come from one death camp -- Auschwitz – to another one in Dachau.

When the boxcar doors finally opened, we could see SS men with German shepherd dogs, batons and large wooden sticks. We were ordered to jump out of the cars, "Quick, quick, get out, get out." Those who didn't do what they were told were brutally beaten with sticks or bitten by the giant German shepherd dogs. We were ordered to position ourselves as soldiers would, in rows of five and at attention. Again, like at Auschwitz, the counting began. When it finished, it became clear that the numbers were not to the satisfaction of the SS officer. Some of the less sick men were ordered back into the cattle cars to unload the dead, laying them next to each other so that they too would be counted. After a few hours of standing in the unbearable heat, some people simply collapsed. An SS officer appeared and lectured us, "This is not a resort. You were brought here to work or to die, you bastards." The officer then ordered, "Marching!" and we started walking.

We had to march at a quick pace to another train and were again loaded into the standard cattle car. This time, however, we were guarded by fewer SS men and mostly older soldiers. Again, the doors were locked from the outside. We all wondered where we were off to now and how long the trip would take. With the complete absence of water, food and rest, we were too exhausted to talk. We were just trying to draw in a bit of air or find a flat spot wherever possible. We stood all night in the cars. The next morning the train started moving again, passing fantastically luscious and beautiful fields and tall pine forests.

We arrived near the Kaufering railway station, camp Hurlach (Kaufering IV), where the train stopped in an open area. Not far away were forests on both sides of the track. Wehrmacht soldiers and other soldiers with black uniforms (later known to be members of the Dead Heads) ordered us to get out of the cars with the familiar cry of "Get out, get out!" and "Quick, quick!" The Germans were always chasing us about with these words and phrases. Although our captors weren't as brutal as some of those at our previous stops, they still made their way around with rubber truncheons and rifles. We lined up in columns, stood and were counted and re-counted until our numbers drew even with whatever list they were using. The SS-Sturmbannführer was, at last, satisfied that everything was just right. We were then ordered to get in a truck for the 8 to 10 mile ride to the camp.

Driving along a narrow road, we crossed an area that was wooded on both sides and finally came to a stop. "Out, out, quick, quick, hurry up!" We took up positions while many of the guards and SS officers discussed something that most of us could not hear. A high-ranking SS officer introduced himself as the adjutant of the camp. He then enlightened us as to why we were there and what awaited us. His remarks included calling us, "Dirty Jews, you bastards, you are parasites of humanity and deserve to die here for all the trouble that you have given to the glorious German people." William Temple, the camp commander, was next to speak to us. After each man was given a fifth of a loaf of good bread, Temple shouted, "Caution! This is Dachau bread. This is the first and last free bread that you will get here. From now on you will have to work for it. There will be no loitering, no pushing before work, and no life at the expense of our country." He told us that we were brought here to build a labor camp, which was under the administration of the Dachau concentration camp. He then reiterated that he was the commandant of the camp. We could bring our problems to him, but he would tolerate no complaints. Nobody ever dared to approach him, simply because we were not sure what, in his eyes, constituted a legitimate problem. We spent the night in our pajama-like clothes in the most makeshift of accommodations, sleeping under the stars with one blanket for every four people.

Record documentation ITS (International Tracing
Service)

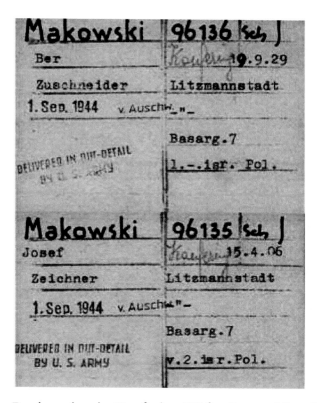

Registration in Kaufering IV for Ber and Josef
Makowski

Chapter 16: Kaufering

Our first day at Kaufering IV started at 4:30 in the morning. After sleeping in our uniforms all night, we stood at attention, ready to be counted. Suddenly, we were sent away to familiarize ourselves with the other prisoners. Needless to say, we were already quite familiar with each other. Instead of working, as we had expected, we were "released." Apparently, our early arrival made it such that Commander Temple wasn't prepared, not having received the tools and equipment that we were going to use to build a labor camp near Hurlach. Many of those who we joined had already been at the camp for a month, cutting down one-quarter square mile of forest then digging up and removing stumps. We saw stacks of building materials, timber and pillars lying around with a barbed wire fence already enclosing the entire camp.

We spent our first weeks trying to dig post holes for the camp's many towers. We also built huts and hauled tons of sod, each strip of which was placed on the roofs to camouflage the camp from aerial detection. The living quarters were below ground level with the roof being the only element of the structure that was above ground. At the end of 1944, the camp was occupied by roughly 4,500 men who lived in the 60 to 70 huts we had built.

Every Dachau sub-camp in the Landsberg/Bavarian region possessed this type of design, consisting primarily of a hole in the ground and an A-shaped roof, which was either supported by wooden logs or square posts of about 38 by 38 inches. Inside, they were fit with long wooden bunks, each softened by straw, for about 60 to 80 people. In the hut's middle stood a wood stove, which served as a heater if we could muster up a few pieces of wood or coal. Improvisation was the key to staying warm, with either sleep boards from destroyed huts or random tree parts used as firewood. The only window was located at the end of the hut, and the sole light bulb was in the middle of the room. It was barely adequate but had to be sufficient for the night, with people constantly going to the latrine. Leaving the hut at night took great strength and skill.

When the ice of winter came, the paths between the huts became pocked with deep, muddy holes. The knee-deep holes made it a challenge to walk. If you fell in, it seemed like nothing short of a horse or truck could get you out. At night, we would sleep with our mud and excrement-covered wooden shoes under our pillows. No one dare leave their shoes on the floor, in fear of having them stolen. The winter of 1945 was very harsh. It seemed that not only were the Nazis punishing us, but also Mother Nature.

Camp IV was completely run by the SS and Kapos, with the standard array of electrified barbed wire fence, barely functional kitchens, and very few latrines. My father and I were shifted around from camp to camp in the Landsberg/Bavarian region as needed. Later, he would work as chief cutter in many of them. The SS and Wehrmacht officers would always wear tailored uniforms. It became my father's job to make changes to them by hand, only because there were no sewing machines. Some of the officers so appreciated the elegance and the form of their uniforms that they asked Father to fashion dresses for their wives and girlfriends. The obvious problem in complying with this request was finding the correct measurements for cutting. Father would draw a picture of the female body and then ask the officer to enter the dimensions. Officers could also bring a picture or a fashion magazine to express their desired design. All of this worked quite well. Father sewed the dress, and the SS officer was happy. Father worked every day nonstop. As a professional, he was allowed to operate out of a small hut. He sewed pants, jackets, caps and made various other modifications as they came up. Occasionally, a few meat products, cheese and jam came his way, but he wasn't able to bring these things into the camp. He and I ate some of the food and hid the rest for other days. Small as I was, I still managed to smuggle some leftover scraps or stolen edibles to the camp to share with some of my fellow sufferers.

The winter of 1944-45 and its dark chill brought continuous misery. In addition to marching from camp to work and back, we were transferred to another location. It was to Kaufering I, the headquarters for the region's eleven work camps. My father was transferred to this camp and it was here that he continued his role as a tailor. Conditions were harsh. Every morning at half past three, we were required to get up and assemble for roll call. For each barracks, the Kapos would report the number of surviving workers, how many had died during the night, and how many were missing. In the case of those who went missing, it was typically suicide by way of throwing oneself against the electrified fences.

This counting went on – sometimes for hours – until the SS were satisfied. We would then be released by the camp commander for work, which might mean marching to the underground bunkers, to local farmsteads or other spots. Some prisoners and I were assigned to repair an old mountain road that went through the city of Landsberg. It was narrow and winding and began at the main square, wriggling and squirming with a slope of at least 45 degrees upwards to the highest point of the city. The freezing weather froze the road's cobblestones, making it slippery. It was our job to break out the old paving stones and install new ones. We worked without gloves, dressed in only a pair of pants, a jacket and clogs. We were forced to wrap our feet in rags or newspaper as we were without stockings and underwear. I even made a hat out of a cement bag to add a bit of warmth to my head. The work took several weeks. Every day we marched from Kaufering I, which was on the opposite side of town, to work and back again. Each trip was four or five kilometers.

German civilians saw us as we were working, knowing us by our striped suits. They either ran quickly past us without saying anything or acted as if we didn't exist. I recall one time, while working on the hill, that a nearby Catholic church gave us shelter after it started to rain. On another day, an older woman offered me half an apple. Upon seeing this, the warden responded like a madman, yelling at her, and asking her what she was doing. He then went on to threaten her with punishment. We were also exposed to the public while we replaced stones on the main square – these people were generally nondescript beings who went to a restaurant, the great church or the town hall. Most residents of the town cared very little about our group of unusually dressed workers, caring primarily about their own lives. There were also shopkeepers near the main square who closed their shutters as soon as they saw us coming. I always wondered why anyone would do that. Why would anyone close their shutters on such a bright day?

Once, we had an older guard – clearly over 50 – watching over us as we repaired some of the steps of the old church. I thought the climb to the church would never end, like ascending a fully vertical ladder on a ten-story building. It happened to be the same church that we sought shelter in a week earlier during the rain, hail and snow when the temperature was about -10*C. I can recall the large paintings on the walls inside the Church and the various statues of Christ and the Saints. How could that be? The irony was sharp. Religion and torture at the same place. For a moment, my mind wandered back to Lodz where, as a little boy living among Christians, several friends called me a 'Christ killer.' Where did such hatred come from? I just couldn't understand it. I was determined, as an enslaved boy in Landsberg that, someday, I would be liberated. After that time came, I would come back to Landsberg and get my answer.

With winter getting worse and worse and food becoming more and more scarce, camp sanitation deteriorated. This opened the door for an enemy which was almost more frightening than the Germans - lice. They were everywhere, in the dormitories, in our hair, in our clothes, all over our bodies. Hundreds of people in the camp were also now sick with high fevers and weakened bodies. It was typhoid fever rearing its head, which I contracted along with many others.

A series of isolation barracks were quickly set up to keep sick slave laborers separate from the healthy workers. The sick were then sent to another camp, Kaufering IV, but didn't receive any form of medical help. Hundreds died every day. Yet, somehow, my father managed to visit me, bringing warm soup, which consisted mainly of water and did not taste very good. He forced me to eat it with a father's persistence winning out over my objections to the taste. I got stronger and my fever went down. Two weeks later, I was transported back to camp Kaufering I.

It was now the middle of February and our fortunes started to turn. Father and I were both transferred to

Kaufering X at Utting, where I remember carrying large stones from one side of the camp to the other. Father tailored and sewed, keeping him from having to do some of the more arduous camp tasks. At the end of the month, we were transported to a new spot, Kaufering XI near the village of Stadtwaldhof. As we came to learn, there was a narrow gauge railway there which led to an underground bunker. It was built entirely by slave labor. Although the work was hard, we could take a shower at least once a week, even if only with cold water. We had no towels and still wore the standard dirty outfit with pants and jacket. The guards were a bit less brutal unless they were from the Hungarian SS, who seemed to carry a deep personal hatred against the Jews. Despite this, I was still compelled to steal food from the SS barracks, located just outside the camp. For me, survival was paramount and food meant survival.

In March 1945, we were informed that the International Red Cross was coming in for a visit. The camp's huts were cleaned, the grounds trimmed and, in at least a few of the barracks, fresh straw was spread on the sleeping areas. We even received clean blankets. The small stoves located in the middle of the cabins were loaded with wood to provide heat. Even a new lightbulb was inserted for greater illumination. Some of us were deloused at Kaufering Camp III. Our old clothes either were replaced or at least dusted with a white powder. We all showered with freezing cold water from a hose outside the building for further cleaning. But adding insult to injury, we weren't offered a towel. If our new clothing didn't fit, we were forced to put our old clothing back on. In the end, most of us got clothes that were too small or we opted for clothing that belonged to previous prisoners. Fortunately, I now had pants that were so long I could wrap them around my frozen, cold feet. And my shirt had long sleeves, which served as gloves for me.

I was also successful at finding shoes that were large enough to accommodate the insertion of paper and rags in the extra space and provide greater warmth. My father worked on my clothes to ensure that they fit better and sewed in an additional liner for extra warmth. He also made me a pair of mittens and a cap. The Swiss Red Cross eventually came with parcels filled with all kinds of food: tinned meat, cheese, chocolate, and lots and lots of goodies. Some of the parcels even contained cigarettes. As the Swiss made their way through our huts, I started to take what I could from them and hide it in my pockets and the lining of my clothes. Just as they left the huts, however, the Kapos began to seize our packages. Many of us, including me, gave them nearly empty packages. Later we exchanged whatever we had left - cigarettes for chocolate or canned meat. Cigarettes and tea had the highest market value. I'm not sure how many huts the Swiss visited nor how many packets were handed over to the prisoners but one thing is certain: the SS barracks were piled high with parcels meant for us!

Gradually and stealthily, I stole any number of items from their boxes and brought them into our cabin.

As opposed to Auschwitz or Birkenau, there were no gas chambers or crematoria at our camp. There were, however, gallows. When it came to corporal punishment, prisoners were typically hit with severe blows in the middle of the parade ground and we all had to watch. The gallows were used for "serious crimes" such as trying to escape, a supposed attack against an overseer or an officer, or some sign of "disrespect" against the German people. During my time in Kaufering I, I must have seen at least 20 hangings.

I recall one day when the commander was so angry he ordered us to march at a running speed until many fell down dead. We were forced to march through fields and forests, sometimes having to run through mud or snow. Those who were too fatigued to carry on were either shot or beaten to death, after which their bodies were loaded into a wagon and brought back to the camp. We marched so long that a guard said we were almost in Schongau, about 28 kilometers from Landsberg. It came as no surprise that the camp commander was rumored to have overseen a Ghetto in Poland and been a member of SS death squads at Auschwitz.

In addition to our camp duties, the SS at times lent us out to German construction companies and sometimes to farmers who grew potatoes in the area of Hurlach, Bavaria and Landsberg. On occasion, a work detail was organized with digging furrows by hand to plant and harvest potatoes.

An additional detail was organized to work at a cement factory. We had to lug 50 pound bags of cement to help with the construction of a three or four-story underground factory. We worked from 7:30 in the morning until noon. Our lunch consisted of rest and a bowl of soup, consisting primarily of grass, hot water with an occasional piece of potato. At approximately 12:30, we got back to work which lasted, without interruption, until late evening. The contractors in charge that ran these work details were Leonhard Moll, Philipp Holzmann, Held & Franke, and Dyckerhoff & Widmann. When we got back to camp, we had to go through the standard count and then received our dinner. Our soup was basically a bowl of hot water with a few pieces of potato and, if we were lucky on rare occasions, we even received vegetables. As there were no seats, we ate our soup standing up or leaned against the walls of a building for support. No one dared eat their soup in the hut as it would have been fought over by a fellow slave laborers.

Ber in the earth barrack (U.S. Army Archive records)

Weingut II (Underground factory) in Igling (in woods near camps)

Chapter 17: Death March

Near April 20, 1945, there were a number of announcements by the camp commandant. He and his senior SS officer told us that we would soon be transferred to yet another camp: "The Americans are moving increasingly closer to the heart of Bavaria. Your work is needed, and you will be treated by the owners of various arms factories as regular workers." The so-called evacuation marches then began. On the evenings of April 22 and 23, 1945, those of us who were strong enough to walk were led out of the camp, most in a northerly direction. We learned from an elderly security guard, a sixty-year-old Wehrmacht soldier and veteran of the Russian Front, that 2,000 people would be required to march the 60 to 70 miles from the main camp to Dachau. On April 25, the rest of us were ordered to line up along a barbed wire fence. Then, the power was turned off and the fence was cut. We hurriedly formed into military-style rows of five, totaling some 50 to 100, and were marched out through the woods to an open field next to the railroad tracks.

To again see the cattle cars was terrifying as we knew what they represented. The guards shouted "quick, quick" as they drove us into the cars. People were trampling over each other. Those who could not move fast enough and fell down never got into a car. They were shot on the spot. At this point, those who were eliminated were primarily skin and bones with their giant eyeballs protruding from their faces.

Those of us who made it into the cattle cars were the lucky ones, or so we thought. Not much later, with the loading completed, the train began to roll north toward Munich. The train didn't get far, going only a short distance into the woods and then stopping. It was the first time in all the transports I'd been on that the large sliding doors weren't locked. Although we initially thought it odd, it soon occurred to us that the Germans knew the exact time of the day that American warplanes operated in the area, trains being one of their favorite targets. Of course, the U.S. pilots didn't know if a train was transporting ammunition, carrying German soldiers or delivering food supplies. Right on cue, our locomotive was hit and smoke bellowed upwards. We could immediately feel the heat and pressure from the explosion. Most of us began to jump from the train in order to seek the protection of the nearby woods. The SS troops were on both sides of the railway track shooting skyward with their machine guns while the Americans attacked from above. People were dying all around us.

Father was wounded just below his heart where the portion of a bullet had entered. Blood started to run, but he managed to tear off a shred of clothing and stuff it into the wound. In the meantime, he yelled at me to lay down and play dead. I felt close to death as a bullet had penetrated my right shin and gone through my right leg, while a bullet splinter had entered my buttocks. After we both regained our senses, we nursed the bleeding and crawled into the forest. Father removed parts of our clothing, ripping them into five- to six-inch wide bandages. He wrapped the makeshift bandages around my wounds and then created a splint out of some sticks, wrapping it tightly around my leg. He managed to stop the bleeding of his own wounds by wrapping strips of cloth around his body. As darkness approached, we dragged ourselves deeper and deeper into the forest, trying to hide from the SS.

We soon came across a small, dead deer, whose belly had been slit open. The opening was just big enough so that we could put in our hands, picking out the entrails and eating the raw flesh. The liver was still warm. The taste of raw meat is impossible to describe. But it was food. From a distance, we could hear other prisoners calling for help. At the same time, the SS was on the hunt for those still alive, asking for surrender or simply shooting on the spot those who tried to escape. As for us, we knew we would either die at the hands of the SS or from our injuries. Therefore, we decided to hide under a pile of broken branches. By the time we were done constructing it, our hiding place almost looked like a tent. That night was the coldest we had ever experienced, or at least it seemed like it. When we could locate dead bodies, we removed their clothes and used them as blankets for warmth.

On the morning of April 26, we heard footsteps from heavy boots, under which cracked broken branches. We also heard the voices of German soldiers. The SS and other soldiers were still looking for living prisoners, shouting, "No harm will come to you." A black-uniformed soldier, or a soldier of the Order of the Dead Head, discovered us. He took his gun out from his holster, pointed it at us, and gave us a choice, "Come with me or remain here." Knowing what he meant, Father and I crawled out of our hole and went with him. He wanted to know how many of us were still alive. Our answer, in perfect German, "Es tut uns leid, wir haben keine Ahnung." (Translation: "We are sorry but we have no idea.") We explained what had happened to the train, how we were injured, and that we were just trying to survive. He was impressed that we spoke excellent German. He asked us various questions: the camp from which we came, which country, etc. He asked so many questions that we were pretty convinced this was the end of us.

Many of us were rounded up and placed in small groups outside of the forest. Under heavy guard, we were led through the fields and small forests toward Landsberg. The other prisoners in the camp told us about the evacuations, murders and beatings, which were much like we had experienced in the last few days. Many prisoners had been killed outside the camp gates. Fields were full of the dead, some with shattered skulls and many without clothes. This is so difficult to describe as I had never, ever seen anything like it.

Dead prisoners after the attack on the evacuation train
April 25, 1945 (U.S. Army Archival Records)

Capt. Paul Jones of the 12th Armored Division - April 1945 (U.S. Army Archival Records)

"Death march" on the new Mountain Road from Landsberg towards Dachau (Private photo)

Chapter 18: Liberation

Later that evening, I took a look through the barbed wire fence at what appeared to be strange vehicles. The front and rear wheels formed a chain-like mechanism, yet it was not a tank. It was moving very fast and had a large white star painted on its side. I later learned that these vehicles were half-tracks. Others followed, but soon disappeared on a narrow country road to the south.

On April 27 at 8:00 o'clock in the morning, the camp gates were open with no guards in sight. The rumors started to fly. Several inmates ventured in front of the barbed wire fence, but didn't go very far. Maybe it was a new SS trick and they would shoot us? Then, to our surprise, appeared a jeep and a vehicle and a half-track that I had seen the previous night. They passed close to the gate. The hatch of one of the half-track vehicles opened on the top and a soldier's head became visible we tried to have a conversation in various languages. Ultimately, we were able to communicate in broken English and Yiddish. We learned that it was the U.S. Army and that, at long last, we were free and liberated.

Some of the soldiers took pictures while others distributed food items including white bread, chocolate, condensed milk, and cans of meat. People began to fight for the food, trampling each other. The soldiers fearing for their lives fired into the air. With the return of calm, we were then pushed back behind the barbed wire and the gates were closed. We just waited. Finally, a German-speaking officer appeared, and inquired about the camp and our group. Accompanying him was a group with Red Cross-marked helmets and armbands. They provided medical assistance. The stronger among us were examined and given injections. For half a day, they isolated people, especially the very sick and weak, ultimately transporting them to other places. The food rations kept coming, but soldiers couldn't do enough for us. The few hundred remaining survivors of Kaufering IV were mere skeletons.

On the next day, the camp gates were again opened with many of us flocking toward the farmhouses that were located nearby. All we cared about was eating: eat, eat, eat and eat more. Beyond the camp, on the road to Iglinger, stood several small farmhouses. Some of the more powerful prisoners, mostly Kapos, started looting, forcing many of the residents to leave their homes. Although Father and I were angry at the Germans, this was something we just couldn't do. I recall coming to one house, Iglinger Straße 3. We asked, even begged, the inhabitants for a place for washing, eating and rest. We were told that they had nothing to do with the SS and they simply couldn't help us and that we should leave. Father presented them with a simple choice – either cooperate or we'd throw them out and take over the farm. In the end, we reached an agreement with them. Father and I would stay in the house, along with the owner. We were given clean beds and allowed to bathe. We took a hot bath, the first hot water and soap we had experienced in a long time. Needless to say, it felt so wonderful that I didn't want to get out of the tub. I savored this luxury for a few hours, or at least it seemed to be that long. Meanwhile, Father was able to find a few articles of civilian clothing including a good pair of shoes and underwear. To put this into perspective, neither of us had worn underwear for over a year. It felt like a dream; so unreal, but true. The new clothes reminded me of dreams I would have during the days and nights in the camp when I would look through imagined wardrobes and select various items I wanted to wear at a party the next day. This was of course pure imagination - illusory, a survival mechanism.

This newfound freedom and a nice bed with clean sheets, a proper pillow and a soft mattress all seemed like an illusion. We just stared at each other, looked in the mirror, and realized that it was indeed true. During the next few days in Landsberg, we explored the places where we had toiled as slaves but didn't venture too far as we were convinced that the owner of the farm wouldn't allow us back into the room if we were gone too long. Food was no longer a daily preoccupation. We kept our pajama uniforms, washing them many times. We hung them on a clothesline and inspected them carefully to make sure there were no more lice nesting in them. My father, the great tailor that he was, separated the seams of the trousers and jackets, measured me many times and then used the farmer's sewing machine to sew me a new, well-fitting suit. This time we did not need any extra fabric or hidden pockets like we did just days before. It was now just a simple, well-fitting suit without the number 96136 on it, a number that had been given to me when we arrived nine month ago at Hurlach (Kaufering IV) concentration camp.

Earth barracks in Kaufering IV (U.S. Army
Archival Records)

My father in 1945 after the liberation of the
concentration camp Kaufering IV

Colonel Silas after liberation by the Americans 12th Armored Division (U.S. Army Archival Records)

on

Captured Commander of Kaufering IV, Capt. Eicheldorfer

(left) 1945, after liberation, Ber and Josef
(right) 1946, Landsberg am Lech, Iglinger Str 3

Chapter 19: Freedom

This newfound freedom was seemingly just as full of adventure and peril as hiding from both the SS and Gestapo. Everywhere we went, things were far from easy with possible threats coming from the local population, the German police, or even the U.S. military. Ultimately, we realized that the lack of documentation proving who we were kept us attached to small pockets of Landsberg am Lech. Sometime in early May 1945, the military government was put in place and things started to get a bit better. Representatives of several Jewish organizations appeared in the city, most notably the Joint Distribution Committee and Hebrew Immigration Aid Society (HIAS). This was in addition to the various survivors committees of the different camps in the Landsberg am Lech area.

When registration started, we were photographed and assigned passports which were, in effect, issued by the U.S. Army. As survivors of the death camps, most of us were declared "stateless." Certainly, while freedom is a great thing, it is beyond difficult when a person has no documents to prove their identity. How far could we actually venture from our temporary home of cleanliness and comfort without an official identity? One of us always had to guard what we came to refer to as the "Grand Hotel", our farmhouse home. However, in time, our newly acquired passports helped us gain status in the community, thereby entitling us to food rations, medical care, clothing, toiletries and all the luxuries of daily life that we had been denied for such a long time.

Several days after the liberation I became ill with dysentery, perhaps because I had fully hit my long-shrunken stomach with so much delicious food. I was moved by a military ambulance to the hospital of St. Ottilen, a Franciscan Monastery located a few kilometers from Landsberg. It had been a military hospital for wounded German soldiers. While there, I saw several former slave laborers, including some friends from Lodz. I remembered one of them, Ben Adelman, from Camp IV, the sick camp or the "Krepierlager", as we called it. Ben was at least ten years older than me and had also been transported from the Lodz ghetto to Auschwitz with his father, and then onto the Landsberg/Kaupering area. Ben was very, very ill, but he assured me that Dr. Grinberg had taken a personal interest in him and told him that he may have to stay an extended period in St. Ottilen.

Luckily, I only had to spend a few weeks at St. Ottilen. The American medical staff were wonderful and advised me to avoid greasy meals and not to drink milk or eat chocolate. This made me wonder what good freedom was when one couldn't enjoy his or her favorite foods. The doctors weren't the only ones with this kind of advice. Father suggested starchy foods such as bread, potatoes, and vegetables. For a man with no medical training, he was on spot. After my release from St. Ottilen, Father and I returned to the "Grand Hotel," where we had a lengthy discussion about what we should do next. Should we opt for the newly organized Displaced Persons (DP) camp in Landsberg or stay in the farmhouse? Because camp life seemed less than attractive to us, we opted to stay at the farmhouse. In addition, Father decided that he would return to Lodz to search for family members.

It was now the end of May 1945. The weather was wonderful: spring was in the air, the trees and wild flowers were in full bloom, and the air was so fresh. Such simple enjoyment of the weather was a luxury since we had been forced to do without for so long. Early one morning I strolled into town and just sat on a bench along the Lech appreciating the flowing water and watching the ducks and nature, to say nothing of the joy of viewing the jumping fish. I sat and thought about my future for a good, long while until I became involved in conversation with an older German man. He spoke with a heavy Bavarian dialect that I could hardly understand. He was a retired professor from the University of Munich. The overwhelming taboo of any conversation was one's affiliation with the Nazi Party. While he was indeed a member of the Nazi Party, he was still interested in my plight.

He was also impressed by my knowledge of German, although he did say that it was essential that I learn grammar. With that said, we met daily by the river and he taught me how to improve the German and using proper grammar. As a birder, he also taught me ornithology. How ironic that an ex-Nazi would be the one to help me take control of my life again. He insisted on the three-hour daily classes, where he drilled me on my German grammar. In good time, reading and writing came when I enrolled for Radio and Electrical courses in the newly founded college for Displaced Person's (DP's) at the former German barracks the Wehrmacht Kasserne.

Learning had come to define my life. It was not long after my morning lessons in Landsberg that -- not far from Munich -- I learned mathematics and physics. I was also enrolled in classes of Russian history with a former prisoner and professor from Moscow State University. I found them quite boring. I took the train to attend night school, moving from Munich to New Freiman, where there was another DP camp for former slave laborers from various concentration camps where one could learn additional subjects.

It was in New Freiman that I met my cousin Sura Tauba, my father's niece. It's near impossible to describe how incredibly happy we were about this chance meeting! Sura introduced me to her future husband – a tall over six feet in height, very thin man with short, curly blonde hair. He told me much about his life before the war but what impressed me the most was that he became the police chief of all Jewish DP camps, an appointment that had been granted to him by a U.S. General. It was difficult to conceive how the son of the greatest Rabbi in Poland could become a policeman! Sura's next surprise was that her sister, Helenka, had survived Bergen-Belsen and was now living in Zeilsheim near Frankfurt in a DP camp. She would soon be visiting New Freiman.

The conversation, naturally, then turned to my father. Where was he now? I began to speak about how he had gone back to Lodz to find out how many relatives had survived, most of all looking for my mother and my brother. We all hoped that he would come back and tell us that the whole family was alive. Being significantly older that me, Sura began to act as my surrogate mother. At least that's how she put it.

Father came back from Poland in June 1945, reporting that he had tracked down my mother's youngest sister who had survived a 450-kilometer death march from Auschwitz to Czechoslovakia. She was found living in a DP camp in Ansbach. I still am amazed by how quickly people could be found -- newspapers in Germany, France, Poland and other European countries provided lists of survivors and were key in these searches. During his stay in Łódź, Father found a bulletin board confirming that another family member, my mother' brother, survived serving in the Russian Army. Upon meeting him, father brought him the good news of the survival of his sister in the Ansbach DP camp. We learned from a French Jewish publication that three cousins of my mother had also survived and were now living in Paris. The three of them, all brothers, left Lodz before the Nazi occupation of Poland and had become members of the French Underground.

Later that summer of 1945, all of the surviving family members met in Paris. Many tears were shed, both of joy and pain. The three brothers stayed in Paris after our celebration while the rest of us returned our respective DP camps or, in my case, to Landsberg. Needless to say, my Father was completely devastated after the meeting. Not being able to find my mother or brother crushed him.

Father and I went on to travel, visiting friends and relatives in the various DP camps in Germany. We even went to Prague to try to locate potential relatives. It was a beautiful trip, but useless, as we found no one. Discouraged, we returned to Landsberg. I continued to attend my three schools, graduating from High school and Technical school, that was my life for the rest of 1945, all of 1946, and part of 1947.

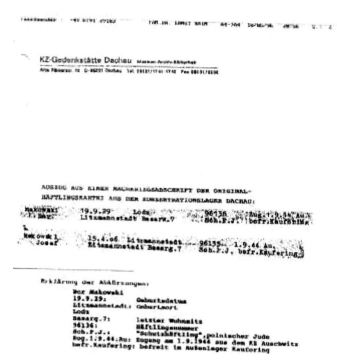

Dachau Concentration Camp Liberation document

Stateless Passport issued by the Jewish Committee
in Landsberg

Ber Makowski in 1946 after the liberation in
Landsberg am Lech

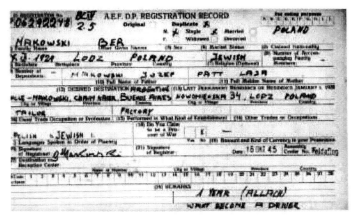

Immigration Record (ITS) International Tracing
Service

Chapter 20: Immigration and Belongings

In the middle of 1946, I decided to leave Europe. Germany was not my country and I didn't want to return to Poland, a place where there was nowhere to return. I opted to immigrate to the United States under the auspices of the "child-quota."

In the meantime, my cousin Sura married Mietek and I moved in with them in New Freiman, a suburb of Munich. With the family's help, I completed all of the required documents and sent them on to the HIAS. It took between two and three months before I received the message that all of my documents were in order and I would receive a quota number. Freiman's HIAS (Hebrew Immigrant Aid Society) office informed me that I should be ready for a move to the Children's Center at southern Bavaria's Prien am Chiemsee in southern Bavaria's Lake Hotel.

My stay at the Lakes Hotel in Prien am Chiemsee was a welcome change. We went to school, took trips to different cities, and even partook in various snow sports. In June 1947, I was fortunate enough to be part of a small group that was selected to travel to the U.S. The first-class cars to Bremen were vastly different from the cattle cars in which we traveled during the horrific days of the death camps. When we arrived in Bremenhaven, we were processed through U.S. Immigration: papers, visas, guarantors, and photos were all part of the process. That was a full day endeavor.

Next was the long journey to New York on the U.S. Navy transport ship, Marine Marline. This was, yet again, a new experience, as I had never traveled on the ocean. Seasickness took a toll on all of us but on June 7, 1947, we arrived. We cried and wept with joy at the sight of the Statue of Liberty, "Lady Liberty" as we called her. At last, we were truly free in the land of unlimited opportunity, in the country where the streets were paved gold (or so we thought!).

After a short, three-week stay in the Bronx, I came to the conclusion that the big city was not for me. It had long been my wish to live in the land of cowboys, as I had seen in Hollywood movies. Just like that, my wish was granted and the Jewish Family Services in Kansas City, Missouri agreed to vouch for me. With six dollars in my pocket and ten words of English in my head, I arrived in Kansas City via train. It was here that my new beginning in the land of opportunity would be launched. I had come to the realization that the streets were far from teeming with gold and there were no cowboys riding about as I had imagined when I was back in Europe, but it was a welcome beginning just the same.

With friends on an excursion to Munich – Ber
Makowski fourth from the right - 1947

In the Children's Center Prien am Chiemsee - 1947

Prior to this, I had returned to high school, graduating in 1948. I then began my studies in electronics and nuclear technology. I finished my degree in 1953. By 1956, I was studying aerospace technology and working in the field, most notably as a Senior Project Engineer developing equipment for the future Moon landing.

In 1952, I married my wife Eleanor (Ellie) in Kansas City, Missouri. We then moved to Great Bend, Kansas, where my official first job was in the oil industry. After a year, I was hired by the Aerojet General Corporation as a Senior Engineer and relocated to Sacramento, California. Ellie and I were blessed with two children, both born in Sacramento, and four grandchildren.

Both of my daughters attended school in the Sacramento City Unified School district, and graduated from Sacramento State University. My two older grandchildren both have college degrees as well – one from Fresno State University and one from San Diego State University.

My Gratitude

As you have read, my father was my ever-present guardian angel. When we were registered by the German authorities in the Lodz Ghetto, his ability to make me five years older made the difference between my life and death. His ingenuity and attentiveness saved me from a terrifying death in the gas chambers of Auschwitz. He took care of me when I was deathly ill with typhoid fever in camp Hurlach (Kaufering IV), and saved me again in April 1945 during the "liquidation" or the ordered so-called "evacuation" of the sick from Hurlach to Dachau.

In 1949, two years after my arrival in Kansas City, Missouri, It was now my turn to give my father the biggest thank you that I could. I signed an affidavit which allowed him to follow me from Germany to the United States. Before he arrived, I had secured him a job in his profession an apartment.

In 1989, when he took deathly ill with a brain tumor, I went to Kansas City, became his constant caregiver, and shared his final thoughts. He died in 1990 in Kansas City. It was his wish to be buried in Sacramento where I lived. I made it happen.

My gratitude must also be extended to my newly adopted country. In 1949, two years after I stepped foot in New York from the ship Marine Marline I returned to Germany to work as an interpreter and witness in the last Dachau trials for the U.S. Army, from 1950 to 1952. I also served in the Medical Corps in the Korean War, and being the Rough Riding Rabbi (See Photo).

Prior to this, I had returned to high school in Kansas City, Missouri graduating in 1948. In 1952, I married my wife Eleanor in Kansas City, Missouri. I then began my studies in electronics and nuclear technology. I finished my degree in 1953. We then moved to Great Bend, Kansas, where my official first job was in the oil industry. After one year with Hulliburton Oil Well Cementing company, I was pirated away by the Aerojet General Corporation as a Senior Engineer, relocating to Sacramento, California. By 1956, I was studying aerospace technology and working in the field, most notably as a Senior Project Engineer developing equipment for the future Moon landings. Developing and designing specialized equipment for the Intercontinental Ballistic Missiles, the Titan systems.

Both of my daughters attended school in the Sacramento City Unified School district, and graduated from Sacramento State University. My two older grandchildren both have college degrees as well – one from Fresno State University and one from San Diego State University.

I cannot end my story without telling of my love for my dear wife Ellie. We were married for 56 years. She passed away April 15, 2008, after which I founded the Eleanor J. Marks Holocaust Foundation in her memory. The foundation awards prizes for essays about the Holocaust written by students from sixth to twelfth grade and students in college, in the U.S., Europe and Asia.

The events of my life, born into Judaism, with two Rabbinic Grandfathers, and suffering for five and half years during the Holocaust led inevitably led me to my adult achievement of making what once I thought was lost.

In 2008, I celebrated a very special passage at Congregation B'nai Israel in Sacramento – my Bar Mitzvah. The Bar Mitzvah is the ceremony celebrating a Jewish boy's transition from childhood to adulthood at the age of 13. The years of Nazi oppression made this impossible for me to do. I essentially had to wait until my 80s to become – in a religious sense – a man.

Today, I still work as an environmental engineer. Retirement will never be my thing, even at 80 years old, or is it 85? For me, age is just a state of mind.

Starting in 1969, when my daughter Leann was in elementary school, I began to speak in schools about my life in the camps during the Holocaust. I've been doing the same in Germany and throughout Europe since 1995. I've spoken to students in Belgium, Austria France, Luxembourg, Slovenia, Poland, Serbia, Hong Kong, China and Taiwan. This educational mission has become a huge part of my life.

As a survivor of the Holocaust, these conversations with young people are very important to me. Our younger generations must understand that democracy and humanity must be protected and preserved with all the vigor we can muster.

Bernard and his wife Ellie

My Bar Mitzvah – 2008

Acting Rabbi, U.S. Army, 1950-1953
Japan and Korea

Note of thanks

This book was written over a period of many years. Many friends, family members and relatives read the manuscript, annotated and corrected it. I want to thank all who gave their suggestions.

Chava Mathe - Herrsching, Germany.

Michele Diament - Memphis, Tennessee, USA

Bernie Goldberg - Sacramento, California, USA

Barbara Hutzelmann - Munich, Germany

Albert Knoll - Archivist of the Dachau Memorial Site, Germany

Peter Koch - Dachau Memorial Site, Germany

Hildegard Markwart - Landsberg am Lech, Germany

Klaus Wagner - Landsberg am Lech, Germany

Edith Raim - Landsberg am Lech, Germany

Gerald F. Ward – Sacramento Public Library, Sacramento California, USA

Denise Crevin - Elk Grove, California, USA

James Scott - Sacramento Public Library, Sacramento, California, USA

Annotations

1. Israel Joshua Singer 1, The Brothers Ashkenazi , eg Munich 1986.

2. Oskar Rosenfeld, Why even world records from the Lodz ghetto, Edited by Hanno Loewy, Frankfurt / Main 1994. The quote is from book B , 1942 , p 79

3. The District President of Kalisch (Kalisz) on 10 December 1939 gave orders for the formation of the Lodz Ghetto, in: Susanne Heim / Ulrich Herbert / Hans -Dieter Kreikamp / Horst Möller / Dieter Pohl / Hartmut Weber / Andreas Wirsching (ed.), The Persecution and Assassination of European Jews (VEJ), Vol 4 , Poland September 1939 - July 1941 (edit Klaus -Peter Friedrich , employees Andrea Loew), Munich 2011 , pp. 171-174 . See also Andrea Löw, Jews in the Lodz Ghetto, living conditions, self-perception , behavior, Göttingen 2006, pp. 85

4. Loew, Jews, pp. 295 ff

5. Ibid. , Pp. 298 ff

6. Ibid, p 456 ; . Pp. 470 ff Danuta Czech, calendar of events in the concentration camp at Auschwitz - Birkenau from 1939 to 1945 , Reinbeck near Hamburg 2008, pp. 850-851 , pp. 857-858 , pp. 861 , 866 -867 .

7. Jurek Becker , Inaugural Address , Irene Heidelberger -Leonard (ed.), Jurek Becker , Frankfurt / Main 1992, p 13

8. The Governor of the Warthegau (the annexed Polish territory to Germany) on 18 November,1939 ordered the expropriation of all Jewish bank accounts, deposit accounts to be frozen and they were only allowed to have a maximum of 2000 zloty cash. Once a week, it was permitted to withdraw a maximum of 250 zloty. A day earlier, the Lodz provincial government in Kalisz headed by Dr. Walter Moser determined that the Jewish wholesalers and producers and trading companies would have to relinquish their entire inventories of goods in the textile and leather industry to the German Authorities. With the adoption as early as September and October, nearly all professions were prohibited from trading in textiles and leather. The Jewish population was left with practically nothing.

9. On 9 November 1939 Lodz and surrounding area was incorporated into the Reichsgau Warta, under the leadership of Gauleiter and Reich Governor Arthur Greiser. The city of Lodz formed a German city district in the Regierungsbezirk Kalisch, on 11 April 1940 on Hitler's orders Lodz as renamed as Litzmannstadt.

10. For the purposes of a proposed "Germanization" of the Warta area in Poland (recently annexed to Germany) a resettlement program was instituted for ethnic Germans from various parts of Eastern Europe. Poles and Jews from the Warta area should be deported.. The Higher SS and Police Leader in Poznan, Wilhelm Koppe, was commissioned by

Gauleiter Greiser , on 28 February 1940 to resettle about 100,000 Jews from Lodz), i.e., to deport . Ultimately, at the end of 1939 and beginning of 1940, the Germans deported approximately 71,000 Jews from the city. Before the deportations, by the instigation of Governor General Hans Frank, who wanted to expand his territory in the foreseeable future "free of Jews", were initially stopped. These deportations went often completely chaotic. People were dragged from their homes without prior notice. Raids were conducted at night, rounding up Jews from the streets, often without any luggage.

11. Bernard Marks here refers to executions during the relocation period to the ghetto. From the 12th to the 29th of February 1940, the Jewish population had to be moved to the ghetto in less than a week. No weekly schedules were posted for the evacuations on the 24th of February. Some families were still hoping to stay in their homes. Some tried to escape from the ghetto. After 28th of February thousands of Jews were arrested during the raid. They were beaten, and deported to the General Government area. On "Bloody Thursday" 5 March 1940, German policemen forced all Jews still living in their homes to leave. A number of Jews were shot by the police on the street. All the others had to move into the ghetto. These acts of brutality were ongoing the next day.

12. After the German attack on the Soviet Union on 18 September 1941, plans for the so-called "Final

Solution of the Jewish Question", to murder the European Jews, Heinrich Himmler informed Gauleiter Artur Greiser about the impending deportation of Jews from the German Reich and the Protectorate of Bohemia and Moravia to Lodz. Hitler's intentions were made in accordance with " A Jew-free Germany." Deporting all Jews to the East " was only a "first step." Himmler devised a formula for deportation to the Lodz Ghetto between the 16th October and the 4th November totaling twenty trains with 19,953 Jews from Vienna, Prague, Luxembourg and the German cities of Berlin, Hamburg, Cologne, Dusseldorf and Frankfurt am Main.. The relations between the Western European and the native German Jews complicated matters. By adding 20,000 new residents into the ghetto, a further reduction of food rations and blatantly intensified the already catastrophic housing situation. Schools were closed and used to provide housing facilities.

13. Chelmno is located 55 kilometers northwest of Lodz served as a death camp and was hidden by a wooden fence to the outside. The Commander of the camp was SS -Hauptsturmführer Herbert Lange, later SS -Hauptsturmführer Hans Bothman. And his troops the Tötungsort (Death heads) formed the SS Sonderkommando, however, the organizational and financial management was the responsibility of Gauleiter Arthur Greiser .

In early December 1941, the Jews of the area were killed in mobile gas vans. Then Jewish prisoners buried their bodies in the forest. In June 1942, the SS opened the mass graves and burned the corpses. They stored their victim's belongings in the village church. The extermination camp was still used until the end of 1943 and re-commissioned in the summer of 1944, to exterminate more Jews from the Lodz Ghetto. Then the SS murdered the last Jewish prisoners and destroyed all evidence of the camp,.

14. The year 1944 revealed that the number of murdered Jews at the Auschwitz extermination camp, where hundreds of thousands had been killed since 1942. A terrible high point : From the 15th May to 9 July 1944 rolled 147 deportation trains with 438,000 Hungarian Jews to Auschwitz. More than 330,000 of them were on the selection platform as "unable to work "sorted out and directly killed in the gas chambers. Day and night gas chambers and incinerators were in operation. Those still classified as "fit for work" prisoners were taken and registered in the Auschwitz concentration camp. They were tattooed in the forearm after humiliating admission procedures. However, the Nazi's could not readily accommodate the masses of Jews even with such a huge concentration camp like Auschwitz.

Therefore, the SS set up a new transit camp, which it had not previously existed. They called it " The Depot". The prisoners were given no prison uniforms, nor were they numerically tattooed. They were destined to be slave laborers in the German Empire and were transported as soon as a German contractor needed them.

Beginning in August 1944, Jewish men, women and children were deported from the Lodz Ghetto to Auschwitz- Birkenau, where the SS maintained the "Depot camp". On 16 August 1944 came two new trains from the Lodz ghetto. From both transports a total of only 670 men were taken to the camp and were given a prisoner number tattoo. Those who were considered "fit for work" were probably recorded as "depot prisoners "in the" transit camps B IIc , IIe B and B III. However the majority of the Jews from these two transports were killed immediately after the selection for slave labor. They were sent to the gas chambers. Of the more than 60,000 Jews from the Lodz Ghetto, who were deported to Auschwitz, the SS took only 2,318 persons with prisoner number in the concentration camp Auschwitz -Birkenau, including only two who were women. How many of the Jews from the ghetto that came in the "transit camp," cannot be determined exactly.

15. As of the summer of 1944, Landsberg, Kaufering, Hurlach, Turkheim, Erpfting, Utting, Seestall and Obermeitingen became the place of terror and mass graves for thousands of Jews from all over Europe : On 18 June 1944 transport from Auschwitz with 1,000 Jewish men arrived in Kaufering, Bavaria.

They were the first group to build the slave labor concentration camp, which eventually grew to eleven Dachau sub camps, housing 30,000 mostly Jewish men , women and children.

By war's end, the Nazi Regime had made plans to institute the so-called "Fighter Staff". These were underground concrete factories to be constructed by Jewish slave labor under the code name" wood pigeon ". The underground factories hidden beneath the forests were to be used to assemble the jet aircraft "Messerschmidt 262". Jews from Hungary, Lithuania, Poland, but also from many other European countries were deported to the eleven sub-camps of Dachau concentration camp near Landsberg / Kaufering. From June 1944 until the end of April 1945, in the eleven camps at least over 6,000 people perished as a result of hunger, disease, and exhaustion from overwork.

Literature

Wolfgang Benz / Miriam Bistrovic / Claudia Curio / Barbara Distel / Franziska Jahn / Angelika Königseder / Brigitte Mihok / Verena Walter, Auschwitz , in: Wolfgang Benz / Barbara Distel , The place of terror, Vol 5 (Hinzert, Auschwitz, Neuengamme) Munich 2007, pp. 79-173.

Danuta Czech, calendar of events in the concentration camp Auschwitz -Birkenau 1939-1945, Reinbeck bei Hamburg , 2008.

Sascha Feuchert / Erwin Leibfried / Jörg Riecke (ed.) in collaboration with Julian Baranowski / Joanna Podolska / Krystina Radziszewska / Jacek Walicki , The Chronicle of the Lodz Ghetto / Lodz, 5 volumes , Göttingen 2007.

Sascha Feuchert / Erwin Leibfried / Jörg Riecke (ed.) and Julian Baranowski and Krystina Radziszewska , last days. The Łódź Ghetto Chronicle June / July 1944, Göttingen , 2004.

Wolf Gruner, by the collective designation for the deportation of Jews from Germany (1938-1945) . New perspectives and documents : Birthe Kundrus / Beate Meyer, The deportation of Jews from Germany. Plans Practice reactions 1938-1945, Göttingen 2004, pp. 21-62.

Susanne Heim / Ulrich Herbert / Hans -Dieter Kreikamp / Horst Möller / Dieter Pohl / (ed.), The persecution and murder of the European Jews (VEJ) ,

Vol 4 , Poland September 1939 - July 1941 (edit Klaus - Peter Friedrich , employees Andrea Loew), Munich 2011.

Peter Klein , The "Ghetto Lodz Management " 1940 to 1944. An agency in the field of tension between local bureaucracy and government policy of persecution, Hamburg 2009.

Andrea Löw, in the ghetto Lodz. Living conditions, self-perception, behavior, Göttingen 2006.

Edith Raim, The Dachau concentration camp outside the camp Kaufering and Mühldorf. Rüstungsbauten and forced labor in the last year, 1944/1945, Landsberg am Lech in 1992.

Sabine Schalm , survival through work ? External commands and sub-camp of Dachau Concentration Camp 1933-1945 , Berlin 2009.